MY FIRST HISTORY ENCYCLOPEDIA

Om Books International

CONTENTS

4TH
JULY

GOOD BYE
CAMP DIX

What Is History?

History is the study of the past. It tells us about people who lived in the past, human civilisations and important events. History begins with the evolution of humans and dates back to almost 150,000 years.

How do we learn about the past?

We learn about the past through books, letters, museums and architecture. Artefacts like pottery and tools, excavation sites, human and animal remains also give us an insight into how humans lived and behaved from the prehistoric times, down the ages.

Herodotus

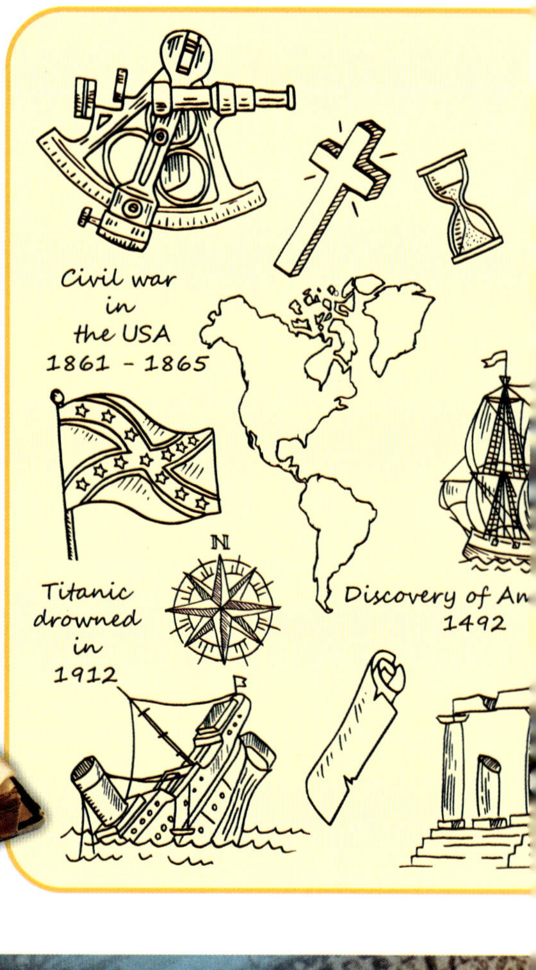

Why do we study history?

Studying history is important because it allows us to understand our past. If we study the successes and failures of the past, we may be able to learn from our mistakes and avoid repeating them in the future.

Who is a historian?

A historian is a person who studies and writes about the past. Some of the famous modern historians are Fernand Braudel, David Christian, Hugh Ambrose, Dorothy Atkinson and Niall Ferguson. Braudel's masterpiece, *The Mediterranean and the Mediterranean World in the Age of Philip II,* shows just how immense a historian's scope can possibly be.

Themes of history

Did You Know?

In the fifth century BCE, a Greek historian, Herodotus, attempted to put down the events of the past to help people recall and remember them. Hence, he is known as the "Father of History".

First Humans

The *Australopithecus afarensis* is the best known earliest human species. It had both ape and human features. It had a flat nose, a projecting lower jaw, a small brain, a hairy body and long arms with curved fingers to climb trees like apes. However, it walked upright on two feet like humans.

Australopithecus

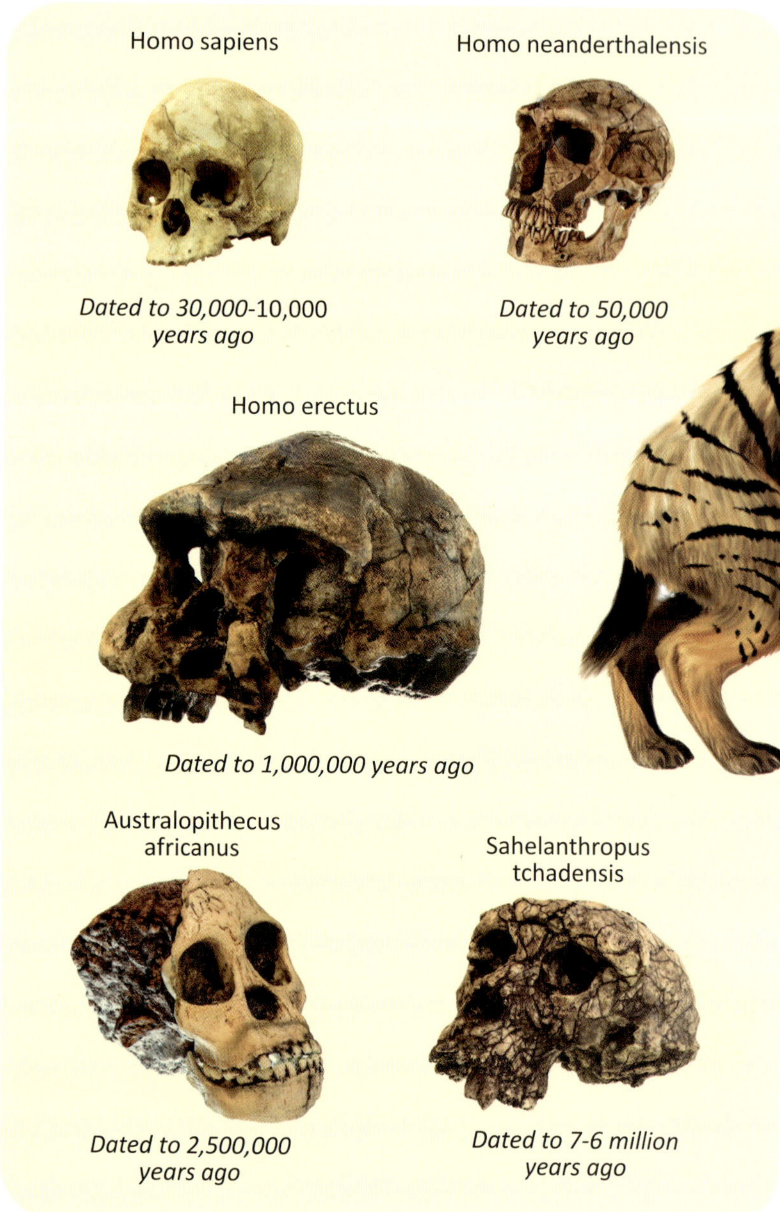

Development of the human brain over the ages

Life of the early humans

Early humans lived in caves. They ate nuts, roots, yams, insects, fish and meat. Gradually, they developed bigger brains and learned to talk. They also lost a lot of their body hair. Over time, they understood how to make fire. Soon, they learnt that fire could keep them warm and help them cook food, making it easier and tastier to eat. In time, they learnt how to develop and make their own tools. Their tools were very basic, but more often than not, they used sticks and bones to dig and also to defend themselves from ferocious animals.

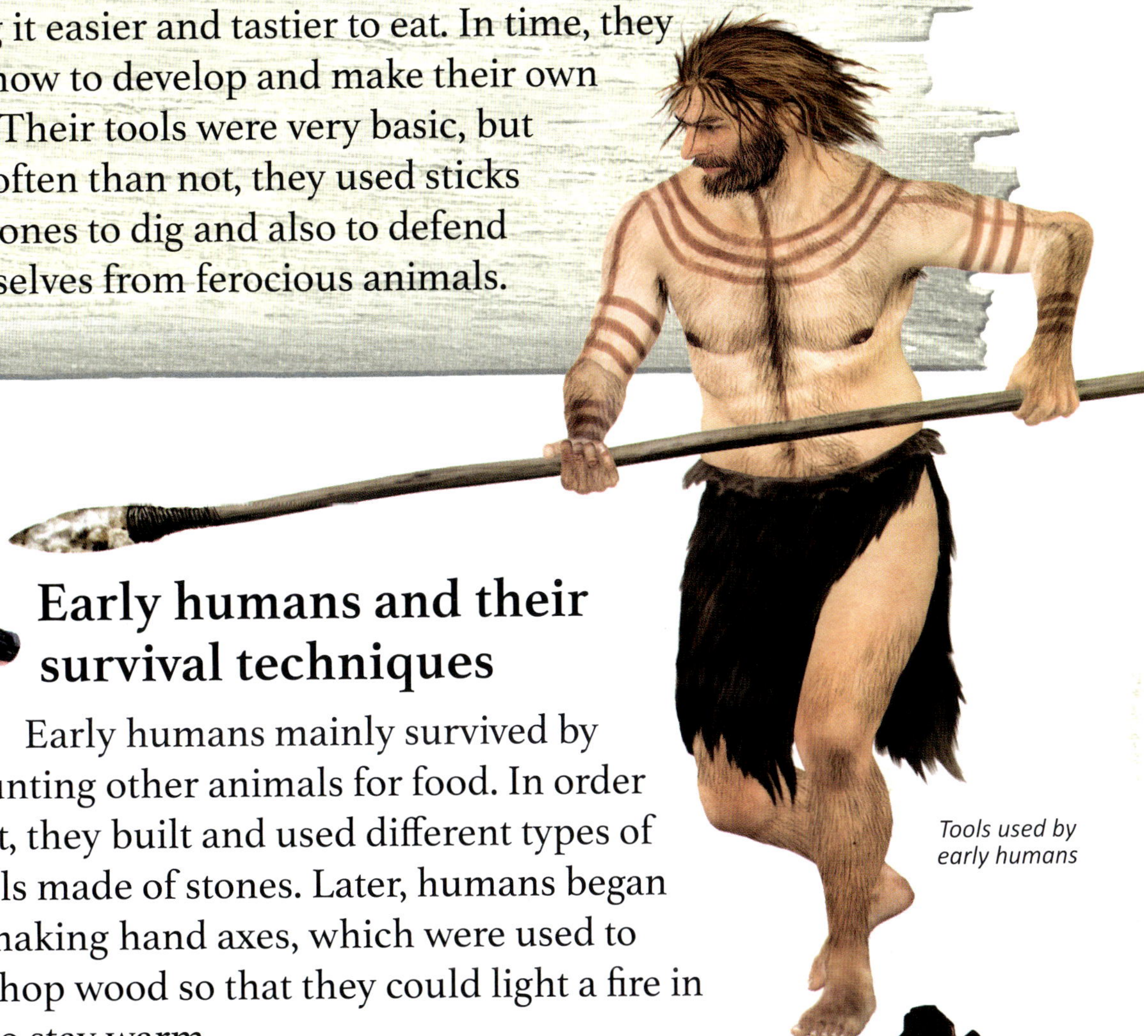

Early humans and their survival techniques

Early humans mainly survived by hunting other animals for food. In order to hunt, they built and used different types of tools made of stones. Later, humans began making hand axes, which were used to chop wood so that they could light a fire in order to stay warm.

Tools used by early humans

Prehistoric Age

Prehistory describes the time that existed before any recorded history, much before human beings began to create written records of their life and of the world in which they lived.

Dinosaurs

For more than 150 million years, Dinosaurs were the main animals on Earth. Some of them were the largest and scariest creatures that ever walked on land. The word *dinosaur* comes from Greek words meaning "terrible lizard". This period was called the Jurassic Period, the age of reptiles.

People of the Prehistoric age

All living beings on this planet belong to and have evolved from the Homo sapiens. Homo sapiens is the Latin term for "wise human". They had developed brains, bipedal gait (where one moves using the two rear limbs or legs) and opposable thumbs.

Neanderthals

The Neanderthals were a subspecies of the Homo sapiens. They lived between 300,000 to 1,000,000 years ago. They were food gatherers and hunters. They also knew how to build shelters and used cleaned animal skins as clothing. The Neanderthals were different from the Homo sapiens in that they had a larger brain, receding chin and a projecting nose.

Art of the Prehistoric age

Prehistoric art

Around 20,000 BCE, human beings had settled in all the different parts of the globe and various art forms—cave paintings, engravings of humans, rock art, terracotta vases and goblet bowls with different decorations—have been discovered from all the different continents from Africa to Europe.

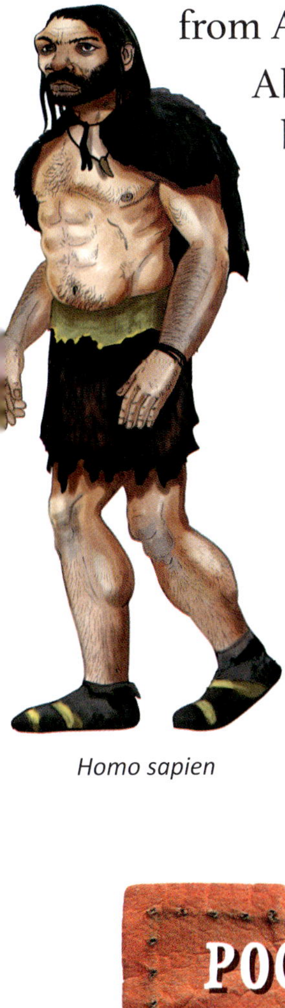

Homo sapien

Abalone shells, ochre, bone, charcoal, grindstones and hammer stones were used for different works of art in the prehistoric period.

Central and East Asia have numerous examples of art with carved figurines found in Malta. The archaeological site of Jiahu in China hosted bone flutes that represented the culture and their appreciation for music.

Terracotta utensils

POCKET FACT

According to biologists, about 1–4% of the present- day human genome is derived from the Neanderthals.

Everything that we today know about prehistoric plants and animals comes from fossils. Fossils are the remains or traces of early life-forms. They are often found in rocks.

Ice Age

Millions and millions of years ago, in Europe and North America, huge glaciers formed repeatedly on the landmasses. This resulted in a drop in temperature, which led to the **Pleistocene Epoch** or the **Great Ice Age.** The Ice Age spread from the North Pole towards the South Pole.

Animals of the Ice Age

There were 5-6 long periods of the Ice Age. Animals like woolly mammoths roamed the cold regions of Europe, Asia, and North America during the ice ages. These animals grazed on plants using their 15-feet-long tusks to dig under snow for food like shrubs and grasses.

Other animals were giant ground sloth, cave bear, dire wolf, diptotrodon, and others.

POCKET FACT

When the ice melted, different ridges, piles and other formations consisting of gravel, sand and soil were formed. The melting caused huge lakes to be formed and the sea level also rose.

Human activities impacted

Conditions were extremely harsh for the people who lived near the ice sheets. This impacted human activities. Towards the end of the second Ice Age, many tribes of hunters and gatherers travelled to different parts of the world.

What made Earth cold?

Scientists have not been able to state what exactly caused the Ice Age, but some believe that the change in Earth's orbital pattern could be one reason behind this.

A few others believe that the huge amounts of dust and fewer gases could have made Earth cold.

Did You Know?

A glacier is a large mass of permanent ice that is formed by the re-crystallisation of snow. Glaciers continue to exist even today, but are slowly melting with a rise in Earth's temperature.

Stone Age

The Stone Age began around 2.5 million years ago and continued till around 3300 BCE. The Stone Age is divided into three separate periods: the Paleolithic Period, the Mesolithic Period and the Neolithic Period.

Different artefacts from the Paleolithic Age

Paleolithic Age

The Paleolithic Age is also known as the "Old Stone Age". Stones were used to make fire and also to make tools of wood, bone as well as of stone.

Mesolithic Age

The Mesolithic Age is also known as the Middle Stone Age. The nomadic Mesolithic people lived in temporary "tent houses" made from animal skins. They used tiny chipped stone tools called "microliths" to make lightweight spears and arrows. Pottery and the bow were developed during this period.

Neolithic Age

The Neolithic Age is also known as the New Stone Age. People used sophisticated tools made from stones. In this period, wood was used to make building and hunting material.

A Stone Age man making a stone tool

The early settlers

Humans began to settle in communities for the first time. This was due to the emergence of agriculture. Crops like barley and wheat were cultivated.

Animals like cow and sheep were domesticated during this period, to ensure a ready supply of meat, milk, wool and leather. Dogs were tamed to help in hunting and to guard against wild animals.

A Neolithic house

Did You Know?

Most clothing was made from skins of animals during this period. In fact, the well-preserved corpse of Otzi the Iceman from 3300 BCE revealed that he wore clothing made entirely from animal skins.

POCKET FACT

It was during the Mesolithic period of the Stone Age that dogs were first kept as pets. Prior to this, all dogs were wild, like the wolves of the present times.

Iron Age

The Iron Age started somewhere in 1200 BCE in the middle and southeastern part of Europe. It was a time when humans used tools and weapons made of iron.

Iron anvil and tools

A decorated armour and shield

Tools and weapons

Iron was also used to make iron-tipped ploughs that helped the farmers tackle hard clay-like soil with ease. Iron was also used to make weapons, armours like shields and helmets, and coins.

Construction of forts and bridges

During the Iron Age, forts and bridges were constructed for the first time. Humans discovered the concept of mining to find salt and other precious minerals. The use of horse chariots was also introduced.

Life expectancy

During this period, the life expectancy of humans was just around 30 years. Villages were made more secure during the Iron Age.

Iron tools used for farming

Emergence of farming

As farming itself offered so many opportunities, everyone worked in the farms and very few chose to be artisans or take up another occupation.

Selling and buying

The Iron Age also marked the start of trading, when people began to sell and buy grains.

Earthenware for cooking

Role of women

Women during this period were skilled at making earthenware which were used for cooking as well as trading purposes. Women also did farm work.

A village house from the Iron Age

POCKET FACT

The Early Iron Age in Central Europe from 800 BCE to 500 BCE was called the "Hallstatt" period, while the later Iron Age was called La Tène.

Mesopotamian Civilisation

Mesopotamia includes areas that are more commonly known as eastern Syria, south-eastern Turkey and a large part of present day Iraq.

Relief of an ancient Assyrian k

Tablet with cuneiform script

5000-3500 BCE

Sumerians set up the first city states in southern Mesopotamia.

3500 BCE

The evolution of writing begins. At first, it appears in the form of pictograms, but it took about a thousand years to evolve into a full cuneiform script.

Map of Babylonia, Mesopotamia

The Code of Ur-Nammu, the first complete law code

2300 BCE

King Sargon of Akkad starts conquering the first empire in world history. The empire reaches its height in 2220 BCE.

2100 BCE

The city of Ur becomes the centre of a powerful Mesopotamian state. It soon fell into decline as the Amorites, a nomadic tribe, started moving into Mesopotamia.

Statue of King Sargon

Religion and literature

The Mesopotamians worshipped Nature along with deities that appeared to meet different kinds of needs, such as power, fertility, wealth, etc. Mesopotamian literature is possibly the oldest known literature in the world. Clay tablets inscribed with texts written in cuneiform script have been found. There is evidence of legal or medical texts, too.

Origin

Mesopotamia basically refers to the land that lies between the rivers Tigris and Euphrates. The Mesopotamian civilisation dates back to 6000 BCE, and evidences of people then occupying this area of land have been found. As the population grew, independent "city-states" emerged. Later, there was unification and Babylon established a state in the south and Assyria, in the north.

Did You Know?

The name Mesopotamia is derived from the Greek words mesos meaning 'middle' and potamos, which means 'river', and it literally means a "country between two rivers".

King Cyrus at a Babylonian temple

1792-49 BCE

King Hammurabi of Babylon conquers a large empire. Hammurabi is famous for the law code which he issues. His empire begins to decline immediately after his death.

Law code of Hammurabi

1530 BCE

Babylonia is conquered by the Kassites, who rule the area for 400+ years.

1500 BCE

The Mitanni (Indo-European people) conquer northern Mesopotamia and areas of Syria and Asia Minor. After 200 years, the kingdom of Assyria conquers northern Mesopotamia from the Mitanni.

Portrait of an old Chaldean man

1100 BCE

Nomadic peoples such as the Aramaeans and the Chaldeans overrun much of Mesopotamia. The kingdoms of Babylon and Assyria go into temporary decline.

Map of Syria

Major achievements

Mathematics, astronomy and legal theory flourished during this period. The move from a nomadic to sedentary life was followed by the emergence of an agricultural economy.

Indus Valley Civilisation

The Indus Valley Civilisation was one of the largest civilisations of the ancient world. It was perhaps the first of the settlements in the Indian subcontinent.

An old map of the Indian sub-continent, 1867

Origin

The Indus Valley Civilisation developed on the banks of the river Indus—Sarasvati. It spanned across present-day Punjab, Haryana, Gujarat, Uttar Pradesh and Sindh and Baluchistan in Pakistan.

Life of the people

The communities in the civilisation were rather advanced. Cities had proper drainage and sewage system. The people followed a number system. The children played with toys made from clay and terracotta. They also played dice games and board games. Both men and women wore jewellery, such as beads.

Harappa and Mohenjo Daro

These were two great cities under the Indus Valley Civilisation. Each had a population of more than 40,000.

Evidence of writing

Artefacts, such as seals found at these sites, prove that the people from this civilisation were literate. However, their script has still not been deciphered.

POCKET FACT

The writing of the Indus Valley people has around 400 picture symbols.

Occupation of the people

The people of the Indus Valley Civilisation subsisted on farming and cattle rearing. They also practised hunting and fishing. Besides, they also traded gold, copper and silver and precious gems.

Decline of the civilisation

Unfortunately, from nearly 2000 BCE, the Indus Valley Civilisation began to decline. This was probably because of the devastating floods that destroyed the crops, or the changing of course of the river Indus, which made the once fertile land barren.

Egyptian Civilisation

The ancient Egyptian civilisation lasted for more than 3,000 years from 3150 BCE to 30 BCE. The monuments and tombs of the Pharaohs of Egypt, called pyramids, which are over 4,000 years old, continue to stand even today.

The Great Nile

Every year the Nile, which flowed through Egypt, would flood. The floods brought in the rich soil of the mountainsides, causing the land to be extremely fertile, and giving life to Egypt's civilisation.

An Egyptian mummy

Practices of the afterlife

The afterlife was very important to the Egyptians. They preserved their dead bodies by mummifying them. The bodies of the dead would be oiled and their internal organs would be removed. The bodies would then be wrapped in long strips of cloth.

The dead were buried with their personal belongings, which the Egyptians believed would be needed in the afterlife. The Pharaohs were buried in pyramids and were given a more elaborate burial.

Gods and goddesses

Apart from royalty, the Egyptians worshipped several gods and goddesses and built temples in their honour. The most important god was Ra, the Sun God. Other important gods were Isis, Osiris, Horus and Thoth.

Hieroglyphic carvings on the walls of an ancient Egyptian temple

Ruins of the Hatshepsut temple, Egypt

Games and entertainment

The Egyptians enjoyed various activities for entertainment. Festivals and games were an important part of their daily lives. They enjoyed hunting, board games, storytelling, swimming, archery, wrestling, chariot racing, dancing, as well as playing with toys.

POCKET FACT

The Pharaoh always covered his head as his hair was not to be seen by common people.

Did You Know?

Cats were considered sacred in ancient Egypt. The house cat was a symbol of grace and poise.

Chinese Civilisation

The Chinese Civilisation is one of the oldest civilisations of the world. The first recorded Chinese dynasty was the Shang Dynasty, which is said to have ruled China from 1766 to 1122 BCE.

A wheelbarrow invented by the Chinese

Mongols and the Great Wall

To keep the Mongols from invading, the Chinese built a huge wall on its northern border. Started by the Qin dynasty, most of the wall was built by the Ming dynasty. It is the longest man-made structure in the world.

Portrait of Emperor Qianlong of the Qing dynasty, the last dynasty to rule China

The ancient Chinese developed a system of writing more than 3,000 years ago. The same characters have evolved over time.

Each character is a unique combination of strokes and meanings. There are thousands of characters in the Chinese language.

Chinese technology and inventions

Printing was first practised in ancient China on wooden blocks. Their other inventions include gunpowder, crossbows, hand fans, fireworks, ploughs, kites, umbrellas, paper money, the compass, silk, paper and the abacus.

Traditional Chinese medicine

The Chinese devised various healing methods such as acupuncture or the science of healing through needles pierced at critical points and acupressure which is the science of healing by applying pressure at key points.

Calligraphy is a known art in China with elaborate and delicate strokes

Languages in China

The many languages and dialects in China are known as Sinitic languages. The main language group, Chinese Han, comes from the Sino-Tibetan area. Other languages are Mandarin, Wu, Gan, Hakka, Xiang and Cantonese.

A terracotta horsedrawn carriage as a part of the terracotta army

The Chinese terracotta warriors

Ying Zheng, the first Emperor of the Qin dynasty, rose to the throne at the age of 13 in 246 BCE. The standardisation of coins, weights, measures, building of canals and roads, etc., are attributed to him. He commissioned the creation of an army of terracotta warriors. This army was intended to serve the emperor in the afterlife.

The army of terracotta warriors

The Great Wall of China

POCKET FACT

Paper was first made in Lei-Yang, China by Ts'ai Lun, a Chinese court official.

Japanese Civilisation

The history of ancient Japan is marked by different periods, each of which left behind a legacy that impacted the culture of Japan as we know it today.

Jomon Period (Circa 13,000-300 BCE)

The Jomon Period essentially encompasses Japan's Neolithic period. It was known for its pottery and ceramics, which had a unique "cord marked" pattern. It is believed that the Jomon people were semi-sedentary and obtained their food through hunting, fishing and gathering.

Remains from the Jomon period

Yayoi Period (300 BCE-250 CE)

During this period, Japan began using metals like bronze and iron. People also discovered newer techniques of agriculture (like wet rice cultivation) and weaving. They began to live in permanent communities.

Sumo wrestling, is an ancient Japanese art, originated in the Shinto religion to entertain the Shinto deities

Kofun Period (250-538 CE)

The documented history of Japan starts with the Kofun Period. It got its name from the Kofun burial grounds that were discovered in Tanegashima Island located to the south of Kyushu. The Shinto culture prevailed during this period and still exists in Japan.

Asuka Period (552-645 CE)

This period was characterised by its strong administration, clear boundaries and trade ties with South Korea. It also marked the beginning of Buddhism. The other ideas that appeared during this time were the documenting of history, using coins as currency, standardising weights and measures, and a central bureaucratic government.

Nara Period (710-782 CE)

This period is also known as the Golden Era of Japanese history. It was named after the city of Nara, which became the base of culture and political power. This period saw its people settled in villages and focussed primarily on agriculture.

A famous Shinto shrine

Heian Period (794-1185 CE)

In 794 CE, the capital moved from Nara to Heian-kyo (known as Kyoto today). The aristocratic Fujiwara family dominated both politics and culture. This period marked the evolution of the kana script, the waka style of poetry, the monogatari, or the narrative tales.

Kamakura Period (1185–1333 C.E)

The feudal era came into play during the Kamakura period when the Samurai class came to power. The royalty became figureheads with the real power being vested in the samurai, shogun and military aristocracy.

The tea ceremony is an elaborate ritual that takes years to master.

Muromachi Period (1392-1573 CE)

The Muromachi Period saw economic and artistic revival, and economic progress. Transportation and urban development were the key themes of this period. Zen Buddhism made an appearance and impacted all aspects of life, namely, art, commerce, education and politics. The shoguns built elegant villas and performed the elaborate tea ceremony. Garden designs, architecture, flower arrangements, calligraphy and preparing and serving food gained much importance.

The Noh dance drama.

Azuchi-Momoyama Period (1574-1600 CE)

The internal conflicts of Japan came to an end with the Azuchi-Momoyama period. By the beginning of the sixteenth century, Christian missionaries made an advent, but they were not too successful with conversions. This was followed by the Edo period (1603–1868) where Japan began to isolate itself from the rest of the world in terms of trade and missionaries, largely due to the fear of European invasion.

Martial arts

Ancient Japan saw much conflict. With the Samurai playing a significant role, ancient Japanese were great students of weaponry and combat techniques. Over a period of time, they developed martial arts into a science, backing it up with deep study. From the twelfth century, combat techniques began to be formalised.

Did You Know?

The word kimono means "a thing to wear". The modern Kimono came into existence during the Heian period.

Karate, an ancient martial art is widely practised even now.

The painted Japanese fan is indicative of the delicate artistry prevalent in Japan.

Historical attire

The Kimono has been worn by both men and women since ancient times. The word kimono literally means "thing to wear". As trading with the outside world began, newer ways of wearing clothes made an appearance. Until the fifteenth century, people wore kimonos that were made of hemp or linen. Traditionally, the art of wearing a kimono was passed on from mother to daughter.

The kimono, a traditional Japanese dress worn by women

FUN FACT

Sushi, a popular Japanese dish, needs to be made delicately. It is said that the blade of a professional sushi chef needs to be sharpened every day just like the sword of a samurai.

Greek Civilisation

The Greek civilisation existed from the end of the Mycenaean civilisation (1200 BCE) until the death of Alexander the Great in 323 BCE. The Greek empire spread from Greece to Europe.

The clothes worn by the men and women of Ancient Greece

The origin of democracy

The Greeks were mainly involved in agriculture. The shortage of land led to clashes between the rich and poor, which paved the way for the beginning of democracy.

Athens

Athens, the largest city-state in Greece, was one of the biggest democracies. Citizens met, chose members of the government and formed a small council. The council discussed public matters by laying it before the assembly.

Olympic Games

The first Olympic Games were held in 776 BCE at the Greek city of Olympia. These Games were played every four years for around 1,200 years, but the Roman Emperor Theodosius I believed that the Games were unchristian and hence abolished them.

Greek literature

The greatest literatures of the early Greek period were the Homeric epics. These were epic poems which described the glorious deeds of great Grecian heroes. The Iliad and the Odyssey are primary examples of the epic narrative.

Ancient Greek philosophers

The three greatest ancient Greek philosophers were Aristotle, Plato, and Socrates. They turned early Greek philosophy into the beginnings of Western philosophy as it is today.

POCKET FACT

Ancient Greeks developed the word "alphabet". The words "alpha" and "beta" make "alphabet"!

Did You Know?

The English word "politics" has its origin in the Greek word "polis", which stands for the term city-state.

Civilisations of Africa

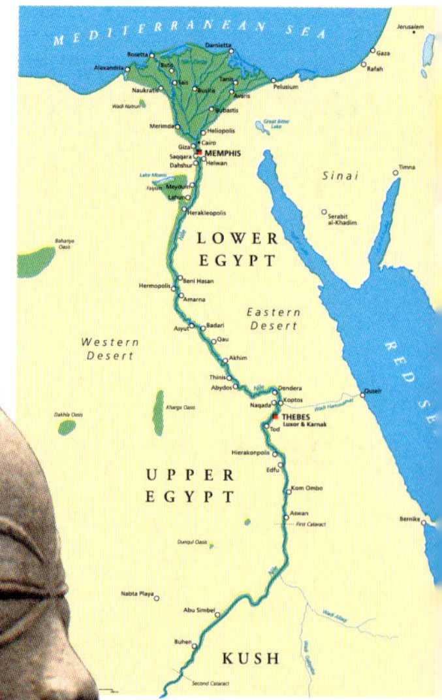

The African Civilisation emerged in Nubia, currently Northern Sudan around 2000 BCE. It was conquered by Egypt in 1500 BCE.

Diverse Africa

Africa can be divided culturally between sub-Saharan Africa and the northern countries from Egypt to Morocco. The northern countries mostly follow the Arabic culture. The southern parts of the Sahara belong to the Bantu group.

A new capital

During the third century BCE, the capital of Kush moved to Meroe, which was on the banks of the river Nile. The people of this region were known as the "Nok". They engaged in occupations such as iron mining and smelting of clay. They used the iron to make tools such as hoes and axes, which they used to clear land for cultivation. They also made iron arrowheads, spears and knives.

Kush nobility

The nobles lived along the River Nile. They lived in houses similar to the Egyptians and worshipped the same gods, with a few gods of their own such as the three-headed lion god. They had queens as rulers rather than kings or pharaohs. They mummified their dead. They built tombs with flat roofs.

The Nok people from the Meroe region

POCKET FACT

The "Nok" is a name which came from the art of this region, which later influenced West African art.

The commoners

The common people lived in villages. They were farmers and were proud of their village. Each village had a leader, but the leader was not a king, queen or chief. The leader did not rule; rather, the leader suggested and led discussions. The villagers took decisions together along with their leader. The common people also mummified their dead copying the nobility. They also worshipped the same gods. However, they did not consider themselves as Egyptians.

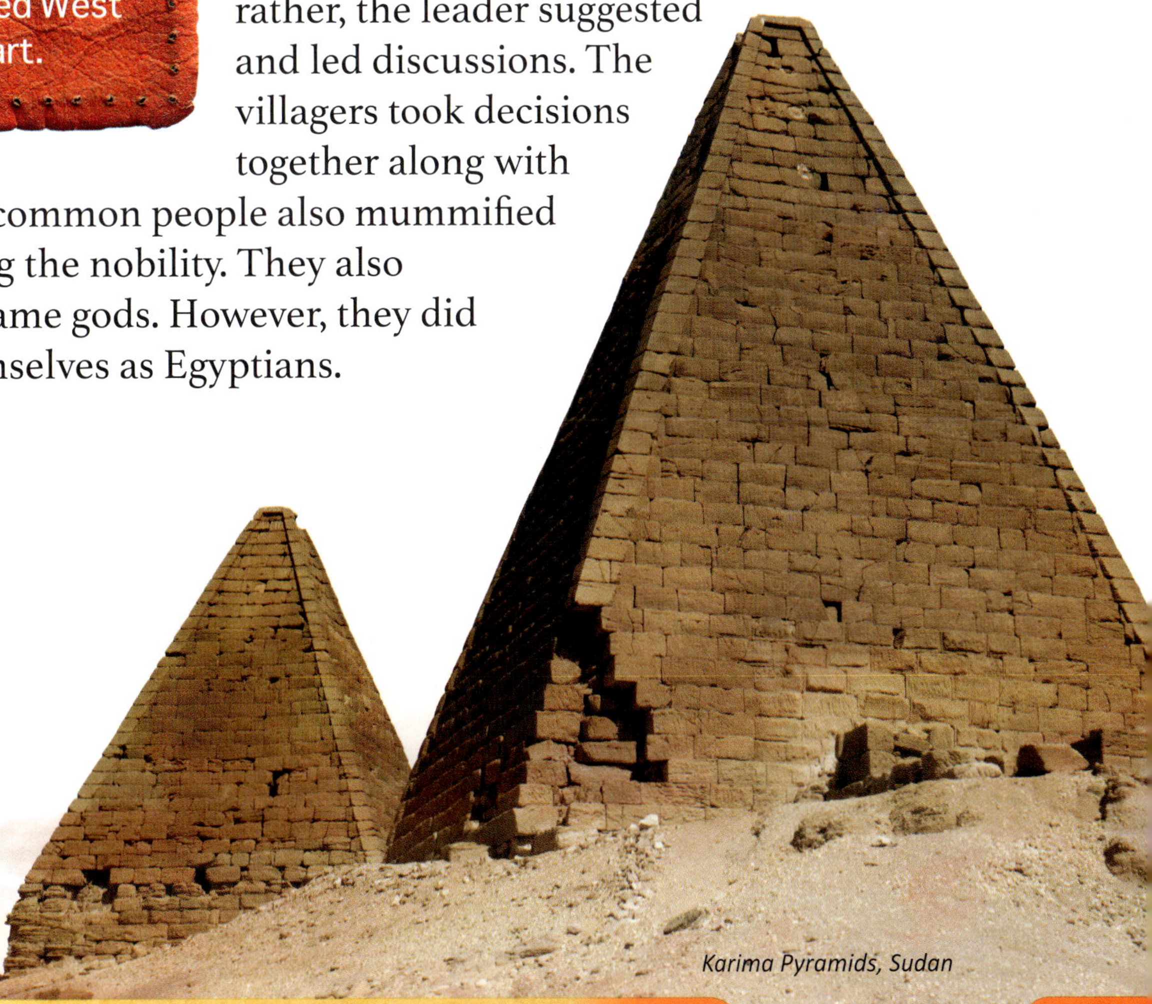

Karima Pyramids, Sudan

Ancient Italic Period

Italy's first societies emerged around 1200 BCE. Around 800 BCE, the Greco-Romans settled in the south and the Etruscans arose in central Italy. By the sixth century BCE, the Etruscans had created a group of states called Etruria.

Ancient Etruscan art

Toga

Toga was the official costume of the Romans. It was made from a semi-circular white wool cloth piece. Only emperors or senators used purple-coloured clothing.

A commemorative plaque

Etruscan gravestones, "Pietra fetida" funerary sphinx, middle sixth century BCE

The Etruscans

The Etruscan region bordered the Tyrrhenian Sea in the west, the Tiber River in the south and east, while in the north was the Arno River. This region was rich in metal ores such as copper, iron and tin. They traded lumber and fur to the east and purchased spices and perfume.

Ancient Roman man and woman wearing Toga

Ancient Italic people and their customs

Etruscan warrior riding a chariot

The Etruscans were known for their gold and semi-precious stone jewellery. They followed a polytheistic religion. These people had a strong belief in life after death. Unlike Greek and Roman societies, women sat with their husbands to eat at banquets. Women also had their own possessions and were very active in politics.

Carvings of ancient Etruscans

The downfall of the Etruscan cities

After 400 years of Etruscan rule, the Etruscan cities could not withstand the force of the reorganised Romans, who had managed to unite themselves and gained over their opponents quite easily. By 265 BCE the Romans had already claimed the Etruscan cities.

Did You Know

The museum is connected to the Archaeological Zone, comprising the excavations of a theatre, baths and an Etruscan-Roman temple.

Etruscan Roman Archeology Museum

Persian Empire

The Persian Empire rose in Western Asia after the fall of the Babylonian Empire. Lasting less than 250 years, it was the largest empire in the ancient world.

Stone bas-relief of Persic soldiers in Persepolis, Ir

Cyrus the Great

The Achaemenid Empire, also known as the First Persian Empire, was founded by Cyrus the Great. His name was derived from Kuros, meaning "like the sun". He founded Persia by uniting the Medes and the Persians—two original Iranian tribes. Under his rule, the people were allowed to practise the religion of their choice. They could keep their customs as long as they paid taxes and obeyed the rulers.

The Great Cylinder

Cyrus the Great was known for creating the first Charter of Human Rights known to humankind. It was written on a clay cylinder called the Great Cylinder or the Cyrus Cylinder, which was excavated in 1879. It was written in the Akkadian language with a cuneiform script. Passages in the text express the emperor's humanity, religious tolerance and freedom. Today, Cyrus the Great is remembered as a wise, peaceful leader and a liberator of his people.

The Cyrus Cylinder, now preserved at the British Museum, London

Fighting the Greeks

After the death of Cyrus the Great, the next strong emperor to come into power was Darius I. Under his rule, the Persians tried to expand their empire by conquering Greece. King Darius first attacked Greece in 490 BCE. However, he only managed to conquer a few city-states, before he was defeated at Athens. His dream of conquering Greece was fulfilled by his son Xerxes I in 480 BCE when he won the Battle of Thermopylae against a strong army of Spartans.

Ruins of the city of Persepolis, the capital of the Persian Empire

POCKET FACT

The name "Persian" comes from the tribal name "Parsua". This was the name given to the land surrounded by the Tigris River where the Persians originally settled.

Did You Know?

The Great Cylinder was also known as the Cyrus Cylinder because its script is said to have been written by Cyrus himself.

Roman Empire

The Roman Empire developed during the sixth century BCE near the River Tiber. Till 117 CE, the Roman Empire had spread to include Italy, the Mediterranean, Europe, England, Wales and even parts of Scotland.

Sculpture of a mother-wolf feeding Romulus and Remus in the Capitoline Hill

Technology

The Romans built aqueducts that could transport water for public baths and toilets. They used water mills, manure and mechanical reapers. They built fantastic roads. Their villas had bath suites, mosaic floors and underfloor heating.

POCKET FACT

The Senate in the USA, which is in charge of making laws there, is actually named after the Roman Senate.

Decline

The Roman military slowly became inefficient. The internal rebellions plagued the government which was unable to collect taxes and safeguard the economy. Foreign powers such as the Visigoths (a Germanic people living in the Roman Empire) also weakened the Roman Empire, leading to its decline.

Did You Know?

According to a legend, Rome was founded by twin brothers named Romulus and Remus in 735 BCE.

Religion

Emperor Constantine made Christianity the religion of the empire. Before the spread of Christianity, the Romans believed in many gods and goddesses like the Greeks.

Antique illustration of Roman Forum, Italy

Gladiators

The Romans held gladiator contests. The gladiators would generally be prisoners or slaves, who would fight each other till either one of the men died. The contests were held in big amphitheatres and people would come to watch the fights. Sometimes, men in armour would fight against animals like bears, bulls, alligators, lions and tigers.

Remains of the public baths in Pompeii

A picture from an archaeological site of Ancient Rome

Mayan Civilisation

The Mayan Civilisation primarily existed in and around the lowlands of the area that is present-day Guatemala. The earliest known Mayan settlements have been said to exist around 1500 CE.

Cities

During their Golden Age, the Mayans built over 40 cities, each with a population ranging from 5,000 to 50,000 people. The Mayan cities had names like Tikal, Uaxactún, Palenque and RíoBec. These cities were supported by agricultural communities and villages. The Mayans followed modern techniques of agriculture like terracing and irrigation.

People and culture

The Mayans are believed to have been an advanced people who excelled in pottery, hieroglyphic writing, mathematics, agricultural techniques and calendar-making.

Ancient Mayan warrior in red and white war paint and golden mask

Architecture

The Mayan people left behind magnificent stone cities, meaningful artwork and amazing architecture in the form of palaces, pyramids, temples and plazas.

A visual depiction of the Mayan calendar

Attire

The Mayans had vibrant dance outfits, elaborate armour for protection and simple flexible clothes for everyday wear. During public events, the ruling class would wear elaborate headdresses and jewellery like bracelets, anklets and neckpieces.

Statue of a Mayan god

Decline

The Mayans inexplicably collapsed and disappeared by AD 900. Their disappearance remains a mystery till today and since the 19th century, historians have been researching the reasons why this happened.

Did You Know?

The Mayans had advanced medical practices. They are known to have performed surgery and made artificial limbs with jade and turquoise; they even used human hair for suturing.

A pyramidical temple from the Mayan period

Barbarian Invasions

Anglo Saxon stone monument

In 410 CE, Rome suffered a series of barbarian invasions. These were attacks by Germanic tribes—Franks, Angles and Saxons—which moved across the Roman Empire in a destructive and barbaric manner, earning them their name.

POCKET FACT

The Franks, Angles and Saxons were originally from "Gaul", the name given to their military area. They were believed to have come from a common background and shared polytheistic beliefs and worshipped many deities.

Reasons

There are numerous reasons that led to the barbaric invasions—the decline of the Roman military, lead poisoning through water and food, the split of the empire and the failing economy.

Franks, Angles and Saxons

These tribes settled down over the vast empire in different regions—the Angles and Saxons settled in England, the Franks ruled in the northern part of France, the Lombards made Italy their hometown, while the Huns eventually lived in Eastern Europe, Central Asia and the Caucasus.

A mosaic depicting the Sword of God, the legendary weapon of Attila the Hun

Attila the Hun

Led by King Attila, the Huns devastated the Gaul region. The Burgundians joined hands to defeat the Huns at the "Battle of the Nations"—as the battle was called. Attila did not give up; he marched through Italy, plundering and leaving in its wake a devastated Rome. Later, the Huns found themselves troubled by famine and plague and their numbers began to drop. Attila's retreat was soon followed by his death.

Painting of the Huns attack in Turkey

Vikings—A Warrior Civilisation

Between the eighth and eleventh centuries, a large number of Scandinavian seafaring warriors, known as Vikings or Norsemen, raided and colonised several settlements in large parts of England, Europe, Russia, Iceland, Greenland and Newfoundland.

Who were the Vikings?

The Vikings basically comprised heads of clans or landowners who, on their own lands, were farmers; but once they set out, they turned into violent raiders and pillagers. They would organise bands of armies, set forth on seagoing vessels called longships and raid coastal cities and towns, plundering, burning, and killing at will.

Longboats

The Vikings knew how to build excellent ships for their military invasions. Their most commonly used boats were "longboats" which could fit nearly 60 Vikings at a time and could land on and depart from land easily.

Achievements

By the middle of the ninth century, the Vikings had brought much of England and Scotland under their control. They established Ireland's early trading towns of Dublin, Waterford and Limerick. They attacked and occupied large parts of France, Italy, Denmark, Greenland and Iceland.

The Viking legacy

The Viking society believed in law and democracy. Though women could not vote, they did enjoy tremendous equality, running farms and businesses while their husbands were at sea.

POCKET FACT

The Vikings considered swords as their most precious possession and even gave them names like "Fierce" or "Leg biter". These were richly decorated with silver and/or copper inlay to form beautiful geometric patterns, animal motifs or Christian icons.

Byzantine Empire

The Byzantine Empire, often referred to as the Eastern Roman Empire, lasted for more than 1,000 years. It encompassed a rich and enduring history and was one of the leading civilisations in the world.

Architecture

The Byzantine Empire presented a blend of Roman, Greek, and Eastern influences. One of the most iconic examples of the empire's architectural mastery is the Hagia Sophia, a marvel of engineering and artistry.

Hagia Sophia

Emperor Basil II

Great leaders

Throughout its existence, the Byzantine Empire was led by a series of exceptional leaders like Emperor Justinian I, Emperor Heraclius and Emperor Basil II. These leaders played a pivotal role in shaping the empire's destiny and preserving its cultural and political legacy.

Constantinople

Constantinople, the capital of the Byzantine Empire, had strategic fortifications, like massive stone walls, moats, and defensive towers, which withstood countless sieges and attacks, preserving the empire's security and allowing it to thrive for centuries.

Fall of the Empire

In the mid-11th century, the Byzantine Empire began to decline in power due to internal strife and external pressure. The fall of Constantinople marked the end of the Byzantine Empire and the beginning of a new chapter in world history.

Did You Know?

Emperor Basil II was known as the "Bulgar-Slayer" because of his successful military campaigns.

Inca Civilisation

The Inca Civilisation came into being during the twelfth century. It was considered to be one of the largest civilisations in pre-Columbian America.

Inca icon

Inca art

Expanding boundaries

Manco Capac, the earliest known leader of the Inca tribe, settled his tribe in Cuzco (now Peru). The Incas began to truly expand their influence under the fourth emperor, Mayta Capac. They plundered neighbouring villages and brought them under their control. It was during the reign of Topa Inca Yupanqui (AD 1471–93) that the Inca empire was the most widespread.

Inca society

The Inca society was fairly advanced. Their emperor ruled with the help of an aristocratic bureaucracy. They built many irrigation systems and a vast road network.

Inca religion

The Incas worshipped animals and nature gods. Inti, the sun god; Apu Illapu, the rain god, and Viracocha, the god of creation were among the chief gods they worshipped. They conducted elaborate rituals that included both animal and human sacrifice.

Inca economy

The Inca economy was primarily agricultural, with a predominance of crops like maize, potatoes, peanuts, cocoa, cassava, cotton, etc. Domestic animals were raised and utilised in farms. Clothing was largely made of llama wool, as well as cotton.

Ancient Inca circular terraces

Inca's water canal in the archeological site of Ollantaytambo, Sacred Valley

Decline

After the death of Topa Inca Yupanqui, Huayna Capac (AD 1493–1525) came to power, but his death brought about another succession struggle. This remained unresolved when the Spanish arrived in Peru in 1532. By 1535, the Inca Civilisation came to an end.

Sapa Inca

The Inca people believed their ruler called the Sapa Inca was a direct descendant of the sun god Inti and considered them as gods.

A view of the ancient Inca City of Machu Picchu, often called the "Lost city of the Incas"

Hinduism

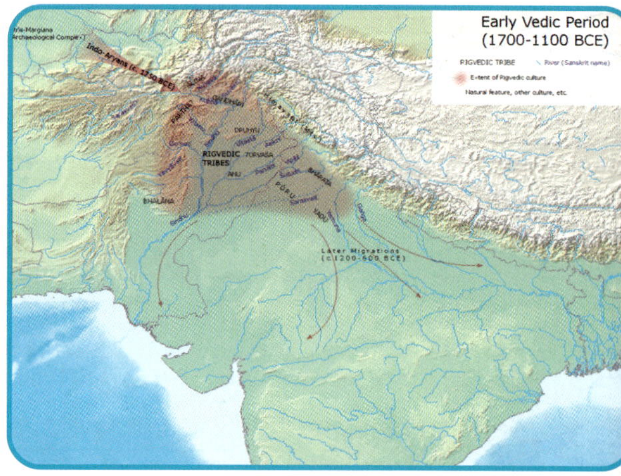

Map showing early Vedic India and the extent of the Aryan migration

Hinduism is one of the world's oldest and most complex religions. Hinduism refers to many different beliefs, philosophies and perspectives that originated in India. It is a polytheistic religion, that is, it involves the worship of several gods.

Evolution

The origins of Hinduism can be traced back to the ancient Indus Valley Civilisation (circa 3300–1300 BCE), at least, or much before that period since Hinduism is considered to be a "sanatan" or eternal religion.

Vedic Period (circa 1500–500 BCE)

Vedic rituals, hymns, and sacred texts formed the basis of early Hindu beliefs. This period saw the worship of various gods, such as Indra, Vayu, Marut, Varun, Rudra and Agni. This period also marked the compilation of the Vedas, which are ancient texts that contain Hindu teachings. There are four Vedas: the Rigveda, the Yajurveda, the Samaveda and the Atharvaveda. Collectively, the four Vedas are known as Chaturveda.

Temple in Karnataka state, India

The Upanishads

Around 800 BCE, the Upanishads appeared, shifting the focus from ritualistic practices to the exploration of metaphysical concepts such as karma, reincarnation, and the nature of reality (Brahman).

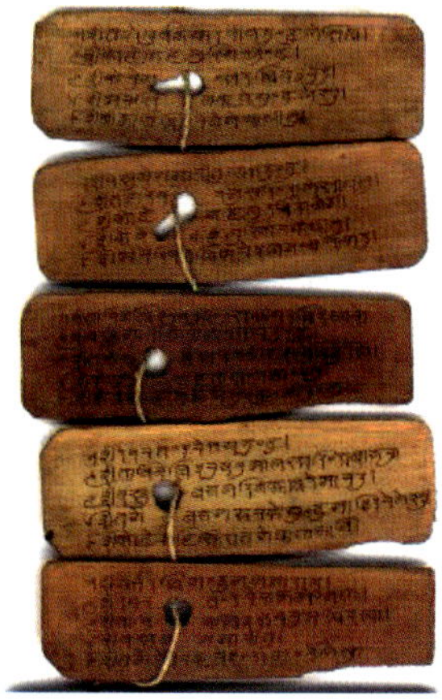

Palm leaf manuscript

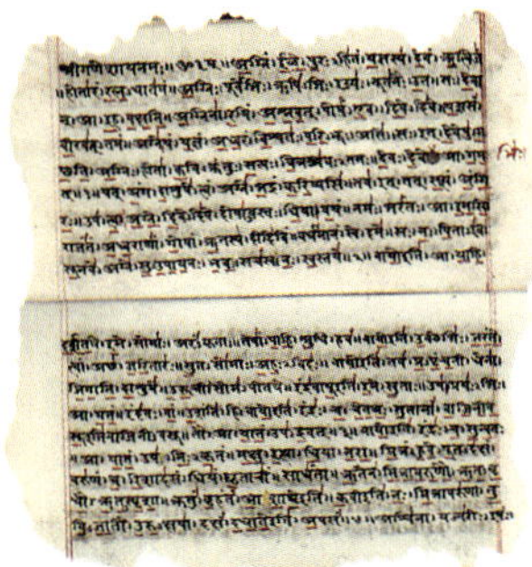

The Rigveda

Integration and adaptability

Over the centuries, Hinduism absorbed a multitude of regional, tribal, and folk beliefs, practices, and deities. However, it never lost its core principles.

Influence on Indian culture and society

The rise of Hinduism was deeply intertwined with Indian culture, art, literature, and governance. It played a pivotal role in shaping social norms, moral values, and ethical principles that guided the lives of people. Today, Hinduism remains a vibrant and diverse faith with millions of followers worldwide.

POCKET FACT

As per the Rigveda, the universe emerged from Prajapati, who is the earliest god and the creator of this world.

Rigveda: oldest among the Vedas; consists of hymns in praise of deities. It contains 1028 hymns and 10,600 verses

Yajurveda: explains various mantras to be sung and religious rituals to be followed by a priest.

Samaveda: considered to contain the root of Indian classical music and dance.

Atharvaveda: a collection of spells and charms to treat disease.

Judaism

Judaism is one of the world's oldest monotheistic religions. It has a rich and complex history that spans thousands of years.

Origins and early beliefs (c. 1800 BCE–c. 1300 BCE)

Judaism traces its origins back to Abraham, who is considered the father of the Jewish people. Accord to tradition, Abraham made a covenant with God, establishing a monotheistic belief system, which was continued by his descendants.

Exodus and covenant (c. 1300 BCE)

The Exodus from Egypt is a central event in Jewish history. Led by Moses, the Israelites escaped slavery in Egypt and journeyed to the Promised Land. During this time, Moses received the Ten Commandments and established a covenant between God and the Israelites.

Formation of the Kingdom of Israel (c. 1000 BCE–586 BCE)

The Israelites established a united monarchy under King David and his successor, King Solomon. This period saw the construction of the First Temple in Jerusalem as a central religious and cultural institution. However, internal conflicts and external pressures eventually led to the division of the kingdom into Israel (Northern Kingdom) and Judah (Southern Kingdom).

The Exodus

Exile and Babylonian Captivity (586 BCE–539 BCE)

Following the destruction of the First Temple by the Babylonians, many Jews were taken into captivity in Babylon. During this period, the Jewish community underwent significant theological and cultural developments.

Moses

Medieval and Modern Developments

Over the centuries, Judaism continued to evolve and adapt to changing circumstances. Jewish communities thrived in various parts of the world, contributing to literature, philosophy, science, and commerce.

Jainism

Jainism originated between the seventh and fifth centuries BCE. It rose as a voice against orthodox religion, which followed rigid rituals and rites.

Statue of Jain god Gomeshvara in Shravanabelagola, India

Rise

It was a time when the old social order began to slowly disintegrate. People began to oppose the complicated rituals and sacrifices of the late Vedic period. They wanted a simple way towards salvation in a language that was known to them.

Rockcut statue of Jain tirthankara in rock niches near Gwalior fort, India

Caste system

The upper caste, that is, the Brahmins lived a life of privilege while the lower castes were discriminated against and denied many resources. Religion was completely inaccessible to the lower castes. Thus, the Kshatriyas, the Vaishyas and the Shudras began to embrace Jainism.

Vardhamana Mahavira

Jainism does not have one founder, but 24 tirthankaras. The twenty-fourth and final tirthankara was Vardhamana, also known as Mahavira (the great hero). Mahavira was a Kshatriya chieftain's son who renounced his princely status at the age of 30 to live the life of an ascetic. Mahavira spent around 12.5 years as a devout ascetic and attained enlightenment (Keval Gyan). He had 11 disciples or ganadharas. He is believed to have died at Pavapuri near Patna.

Principles of Jainism

As per Jainism, right knowledge, right faith and right conduct can help a person attain moksha. For this, the five great vows—non-violence (ahimsa), truth (satya), non-stealing (asteya), celibacy (brahmacharya) and non-attachment (aparigraha)—should be followed.

Carvings in a Jain temple in Ranakpur, India

Hutheesing Jain Temple, constructed in 1848 AD, is one of the best known Jain temples and is located in Gujarat, India

Tirthankaras

The word 'tirthankara' means a teacher who has surmounted the cycle of birth and death, and who shows others the path to attain moksha (salvation).

Chaumukha Mandir–Jain Temple, Ranakpur, India.

Buddhism

Buddhism originated about 2,500 years ago in India. It aims to achieve *nirvana* by following the path laid down by Gautam Buddha. It is believed that if we do good in this life, we will have a better life when we are reborn. Although Buddhism originated in India, it presently has more followers in countries like Thailand, Japan and China.

Buddhist monks praying

Young Buddhist novices pray at Shwezigon Pagoda near Bagan

Gautam Buddha

Gautam Buddha was the founder of Buddhism. His real name was Siddhartha and he renounced his life as a prince after witnessing human suffering.

Becoming the Buddha

At the age of 35, he meditated under the Bodhi tree and gained enlightenment; thus becoming the Buddha (the awakened one).

Old Buddhist Temple Wat Yai Chai Mongkhon in Ayutthaya Province, Thailand

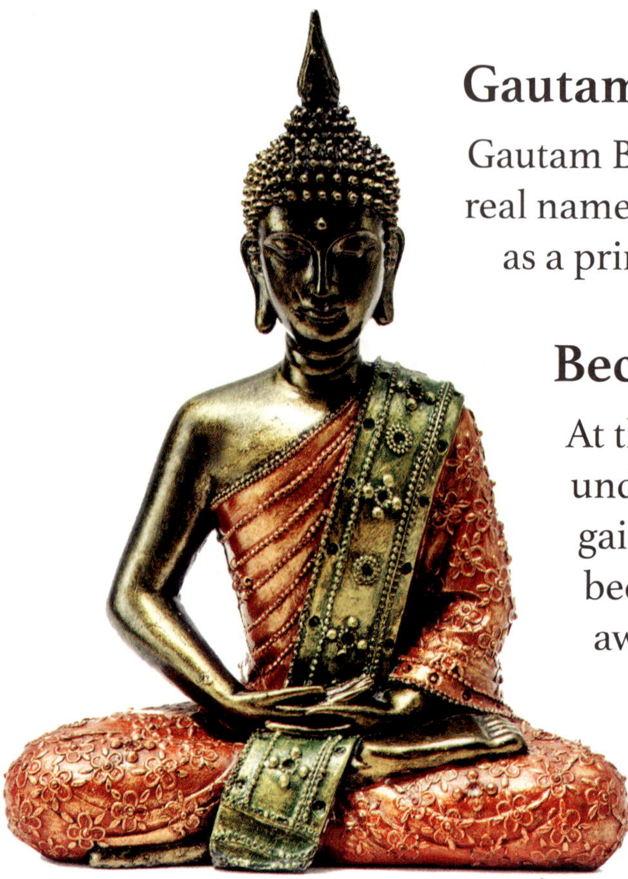

Red and golden Buddha statue

Ashoka

The Mauryan Emperor Ashoka was a follower of Buddhism. He built several Buddhist monuments, such as stupas, sangharamas, viharas and chaityas. Ashoka used oral announcements to spread Buddha's teachings and also had them inscribed on rocks and pillars at various sites, such as Sarnath.

Tibetan prayer wheels in a Buddhist temple

Eightfold path

The Buddha prescribed the eightfold path to end suffering. It includes right views, right intention, right speech, right action, right livelihood, right effort, right concentration and right mindfulness of the Buddhist Sangha or community of monks.

Did You Know?

Gautam Buddha's wife Yashodhara and son Rahul also joined the Buddhist sangha or monastic community.

Four noble truths of Buddhism

Buddhism revolves around the four noble truths: (1) suffering, (2) origin or cause of suffering, (3) cessation of suffering and (4) the path to the cessation of suffering.

First sermon at Sarnath

Gautam Buddha delivered his first sermon at Sarnath to five monks. This was the beginning of the Buddhist Sangha or community of monks.

The Buddhist Council

Ashoka organised the Third Buddhist Council and supported Buddhist missions that travelled as far as Greece, Egypt and Syria. Due to his efforts, the religion gained prominence, particularly after he made Buddhism his state religion.

POCKET FACT

The pink lotus is the supreme lotus, which is generally reserved for the enlightened one or Buddha. The white lotus symbolises the Bodhi or the awakened state.

Taoism

Laozi, the founder of Taoism

Taoism, also known as Daoism, is a philosophical and spiritual tradition that originated in ancient China. Its rise can be traced back to the Eastern Zhou period (770–221 BCE), a time of significant intellectual and cultural ferment in Chinese history.

Rise of Taoism

The development of Taoism was influenced by various thinkers and texts. One of the most significant contributors to the rise of Taoism was Laozi, traditionally considered the founder of the philosophy.

Yin and yang

Yin and yang is a Chinese philosophical concept that describes opposite but interconnected forces. This concept was introduced by Taoism. It represented the dualistic nature of existence and the interplay of opposites.

Laozi

Nature and harmony

Taoism places a strong emphasis on aligning oneself with the natural order of the univers and achieving harmony with it. This idea resonated with people seeking a sense of balance and tranquillity in a rapidly changing and often chaotic world.

Yin and Yang

Rejection of formalism

Taoism emerged in response to the rigid social norms, rituals, and Confucian teachings prevalent during its time. Taoist thought advocated for spontaneity, simplicity, and a rejection of excessive formalism.

Literary and artistic influence

Taoism had a significant impact on Chinese literature, art, and culture. Its emphasis on spontaneity and connection with nature influenced poets, painters, and scholars who contributed to the development of distinct artistic styles. Over the centuries, Taoism transformed from a philosophical school into a multifaceted tradition encompassing spirituality, religion, and cultural influence that continues to resonate with people both within and beyond China.

Did You Know?

"Tao Te Ching" (also spelled "Dao De Jing") is a foundational text that presents the central concepts of Taoism. It was written by Laozi.

Immortality and inner alchemy

As Taoism developed, it incorporated ideas of physical and spiritual immortality. Taoist practitioners explored techniques like meditation, breathing exercises, and herbal remedies, which were aimed at cultivating longevity and spiritual enlightenment.

Christianity

Christianity emerged from the teachings of Jesus Christ and spread throughout the Roman Empire and beyond in the 1st century CE. It grew to become one of the world's major religions, shaping cultures, societies, and civilisations over centuries.

The birth of Jesus

Jewish background

The roots of Christianity are intertwined with Judaism. Jesus Christ, considered the central figure, was born in Bethlehem, part of the Roman province of Judea, around the turn of the 1st century CE.

Life and ministry of Jesus

Jesus preached the message of love, forgiveness, and salvation. His teachings emphasised spiritual and moral principles, challenging established religious norms. His miracles gained him a following and sparked controversy among Jewish leaders who accused him of blasphemy.

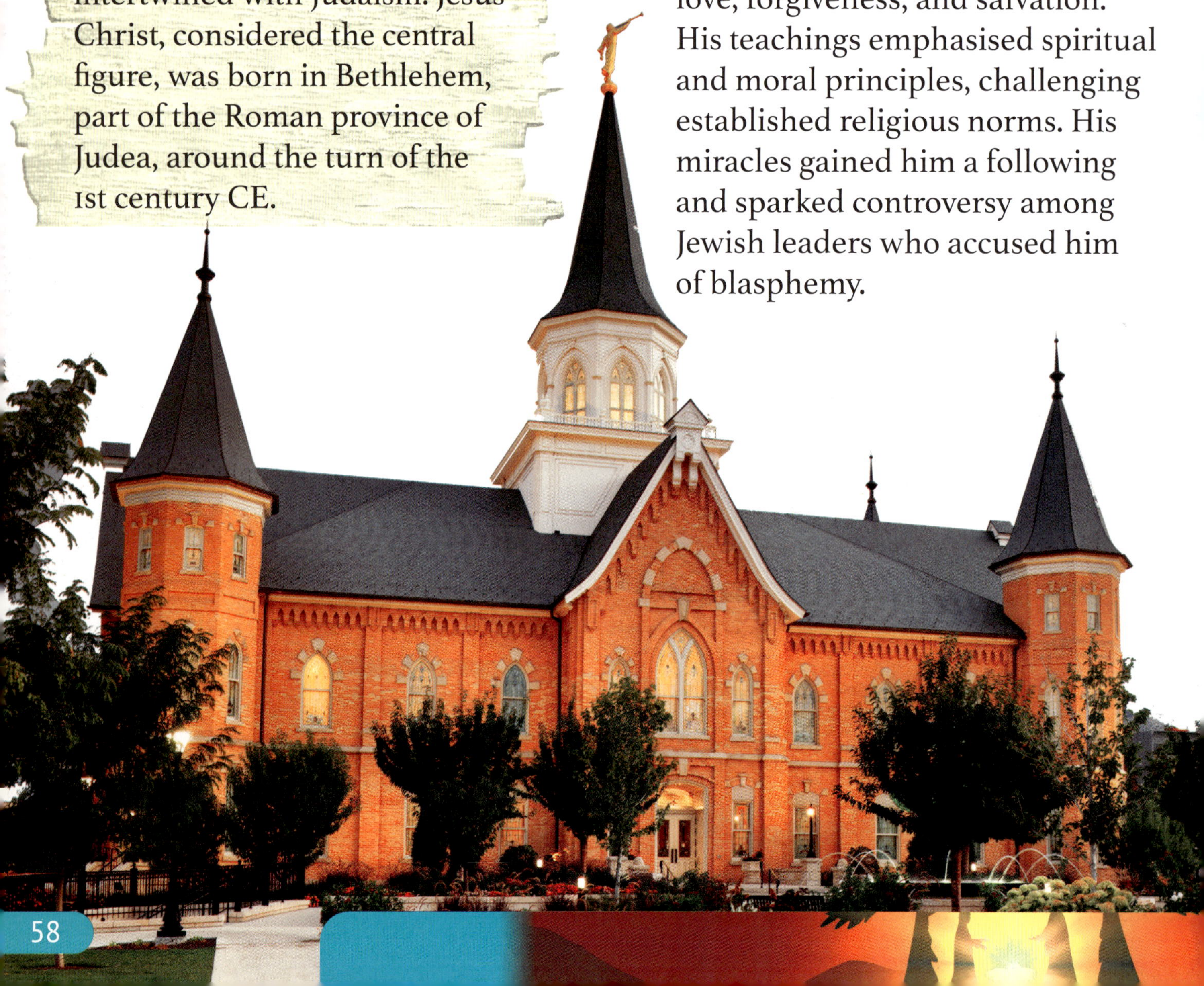

Crucifixion and Resurrection

The events of Jesus's arrest, trial, crucifixion, and subsequent resurrection are central to Christian belief. His crucifixion and resurrection are seen as a sacrifice for humanity's sins, offering salvation and eternal life.

Did You Know?

The Bible, the holy book of the Christians, was originally written in three languages—Hebrew, Aramaic, and Greek. The Bible has been translated into 724 languages.

Early spread and persecutions

After Jesus' death, his followers, known as disciples or apostles, continued his teachings. Christians faced persecution from both Jewish and Roman authorities due to their refusal to worship Roman gods and the emperor.

Later expansion

Emperor Constantine's conversion to Christianity ended Christian persecution and allowed the faith to flourish. Christianity spread throughout Europe, often alongside political conquests. European exploration and colonisation spread Christianity to the Americas, Africa, and Asia.

A global faith

The rise of Christianity from its humble origins in the Roman province of Judea to its status as a global faith is a testament to its enduring appeal and message. Its teachings have left an indelible mark on humanity's spiritual and cultural landscape.

Islam

After Prophet Mohammad's death in 632 CE, the Muslim armies captured large parts of the Middle Eastern cities like Baghdad, Damascus and Cairo. All of these were ruled by the Caliph. The Islamic world was created during the seventh and eighth century Arab conquests, and Islam spread far and wide from Turkey and the Middle East to India.

Prophet Mohammad's stamp

The new Caliph

After the death of Prophet Mohammed, the united tribes of Arabia and the followers of Islam were faced with a dilemma about who would be their next leader. They had two people to choose from. One was Ali, Prophet Mohammed's cousin and son-in-law. The other was Prophet Mohammed's father-in-law and longtime friend, Abu Bakr. The latter received support from many of the elders and he was chosen to become the first Caliph of Islam. Although Abu Bakr died two years later, he managed to convert the entire Arabian Peninsula to Islam with his words, knowledge and wisdom.

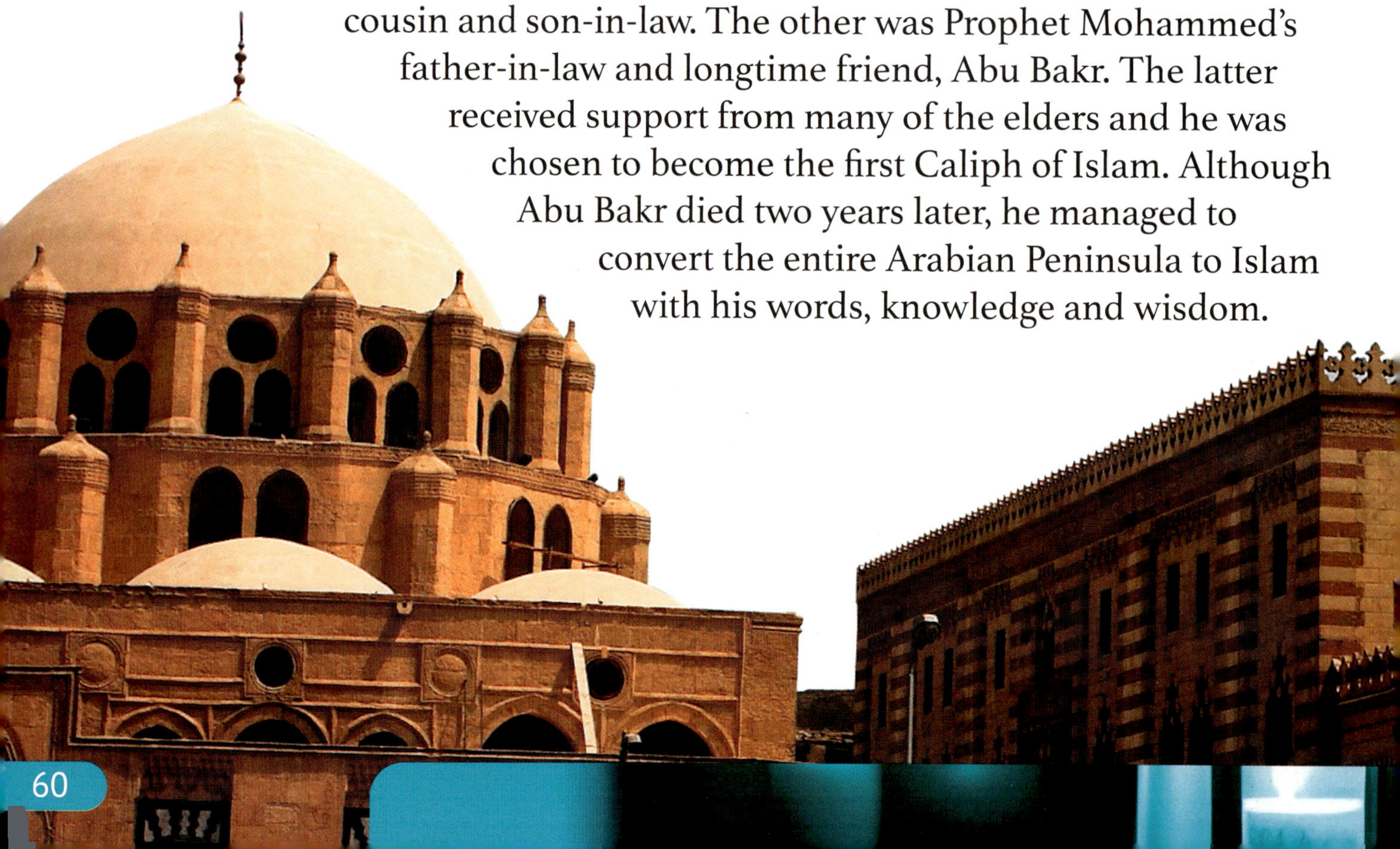

Concerns of the Church

The rise of Islam brought forth concerns among the people of the Catholic Church who began to authorise military crusades against the Muslims. These began in 1095 when Pope Urban II urged the Christian Army to fight its way to Jerusalem. While no one won the crusade, it did bring about a feeling of purpose to the Catholic communities.

Did You Know?

Islam has seven different sects namely Sunni, Shia, Wahabi, Salafi, Barelvi, Sufi and Deobandi each of which has different perspectives.

POCKET FACT

During this period, great works of Greek, Indian and Iranian origin were translated into Arabic. The words like "algebra", "magazine" and "orange" have their roots in the Arabic language.

Sikhism

Sikhism emerged in the Indian subcontinent during a time of social and religious turmoil in the late 15th century. It was founded by Guru Nanak Dev, the first Guru of the Sikhs.

Guru Nanak Dev

Early years

Guru Nanak Dev was the founder and first guru (spiritual leader) of Sikhism. His teachings emphasised the concept of one God, rejected caste-based hierarchies, and stressed the importance of living a morally upright life.

The ten gurus and developmen of Sikh identity

After Guru Nanak's death, a succession of nine gurus followed, each contributing to the development and consolidation of the Sikh doctrine and identity. The compilatior of Guru Granth Sahib, the central religious scripture of Sikhism, was completed under the guidance of Guru Arjan Dev.

Resistance to social injustice

Sikhism emerged as a powerful force against societal inequalities and oppression. The sixth guru, Guru Hargobind Sahib, encouraged Sikhs to defend themselves and stand against tyranny, leading to the militarisation of the community. Guru Gobind Singh, the tenth and final guru, further strengthened Sikh identity by establishing the Khalsa.

Did You Know?

The Guru Granth Sahib contains hymns and writings not only by Sikh gurus but also by saints and poets from diverse backgrounds, reflecting the inclusive nature of Sikhism.

Modern challenges and global reach

The 18th and 19th centuries saw Sikhism face challenges, including persecution by Mughal rulers and later, by British colonial authorities. Despite these difficulties, Sikh communities have thrived and spread across the globe. Today, Sikhism is recognised for its strong emphasis on humanitarian values, community service, and social welfare initiatives.

Golden Temple

Norman Conquest

The Norman ships carrying horses

In AD 1066, William the Conqueror and his army defeated King Harold in the Battle of Hastings. There was a shift of power from the Anglo-Saxons to the Normans.

The Normans

The Normans were Vikings who had settled along the coast of France where they were known as the "Norseman from Norway". Eventually, they came to be known as the "Normans" after they settled down in Normandy.

William the Conqueror

King William I of England, popularly known as William the Conqueror, was the first Norman king of England. King William introduced the tradition of building castles. He ensured the supremacy of the Church in England.

Domesday Book

King William is also credited with having altered land tenures. The Domesday Book which he ordered is a grand survey with details of land ownership and census. It helps assess England's wealth to assist the tax system. Close to 13,000 places were covered in the book, which shows how advanced their methods and technologies must have been.

Detail of the famous Bayeux Tapestry depicting the Norman invasion of England

Bayeux Tapestry

It was a large embroidery made up of small stitches that showcased the events of the Battle of Hastings. It was made by the Normans to mark their victory in the battle.

Art during the Norman legacy

The Normans were great organisers and excellent city planners. They were patrons of art and music. The Norman architectural style can be seen in cathedrals across Ely and Durham in England. It was in the Norman legacy that Latin as a language was introduced.

POCKET FACT

William the Conqueror was illiterate and could not speak English. In fact, after his invasion, French was the preferred language in the courts.

Magna Carta

The Magna Carta was signed in 1215 between King John and the Barons of England. This royal-sealed document was looked upon as one of the most important documents of medieval England as it would bring a stop to the abuse of the king's power.

Doors of the Milan Cathedral depicting conquest of Jerusalem by crusaders

Language

The Magna Carta was written in Medieval Latin on parchment paper. The writing was made by scraping a sharp knife against dry parchment. As this process and paper was expensive, scribes would abbreviate words and write in small letters.

Magna Carta Memorial at Runnymede, Surrey, England, UK

Magna Carta Libertatum, is an English legal charter that required King John of England to proclaim certain rights, respect certain legal procedures and accept that his will could be bound by the law.

Magna Carta of King John, AD 1215

Clauses

The Magna Carta had 63 clauses that outlined the laws which the barons wanted the king to put into practice. The rights included the church rights, the ability to avail justice quickly, no imposition of new taxes without agreement from the barons, feudal payment limits, and so on.

It contained a series of promises to the subjects of England, on the King governing the land, and people, as per the feudal law.

A symbol of the rule of law

The Magna Carta became a symbol of the rule of law as the ultimate sovereign. If there was a corrupt king, these laws could limit his word or could overthrow him.

Although not entirely successful in its aims, the charter did permit further constitutional developments in England in subsequent centuries and it provided inspiration for similar models of limited monarchy in other European states.

Magna Carta

Shield of King John (XIV century)

POCKET FACT

The Magna Carta imposed a limit on royalty and made it amply clear that even the king was below the law.

The Magna Carta being signed by King John, 1215

Europe in Darkness

King of England, Henry V

After the fall of the Western Roman Empire, Europe remained in 'darkness' as it was marked by economic, intellectual and cultural decline.

The Hundred Years' War (1337–1453)

The conflict between the kingdoms of France and England, which actually lasted for 116 years, made things quite difficult for the people. In the backdrop of the terrible wars between the kingdoms of France, the climate had taken its toll on farming and the scarcity of grain led to acute starvation. Around 15 per cent of the population suffered and finally succumbed to diseases like bronchitis, tuberculosis and pneumonia.

The Battle of Crecy, Edward III of Engl
defeats Philip VI of France, 26 August 1

Black Death

The Black Death was the name given to the pandemic that spread across Europe from 1347 to 1350. At the time, the plague was a disease that had no cure and unfortunately was very contagious. The carriers of the disease were essentially fleas that travelled with or lived on the bodies of rats. As the plague began to hit a large number of the population, it spread panic among the peopl who mostly experienced nose bleeds and began to grow pale experiencing swellings in the groin and armpit.

Artist's imagination of the Black Death

Joan of Arc

In 1428, as the English began to invade Southern France, a peasant girl called Joan of Arc decided to battle it out with the forces based on a vision she had from God. She showed exemplary courage and won the battle at Orleans in 1429. She even remained unbeaten in many such victories until she was captured by the Burgundians who sold her to the English and they executed her.

Did You Know?

Plague is an infectious fever caused by bacteria that is passed from rodents to humans via the bite of infected fleas. There was a plague epidemic in India in 1994, in Surat, Gujarat. It claimed 52 lives.

POCKET FACT

During the Middle Ages, animals too were tried for smaller crimes. Sometimes locusts and mice were charged with the crime of spoiling crops or eating the agricultural produce.

Renaissance

The Renaissance emerged in Europe during the late fourteenth century, when there was a rebirth and a reawakening of philosophy, literature and particularly art.

The Concept of Humanism

During the Renaissance, many European thinkers moved away from the Church and promoted investigation and observation. This aspect was called “humanism”.

The Arts Movement

During this time, a lot of religious artwork was made for churches and chapels. However, artists also started getting inspired by Greek and Roman mythology and began developing portraits of real people. Michelangelo, Raphael and Leonardo da Vinci were some of the famous artists of this period.

A building inspired by Renaissance architecture

Literature

The Gutenberg Press invented by Johannes Gutenberg was the first movable printing press. People began to translate and share great works for the education of the masses. Niccolò Machiavelli's *The Prince* was a handbook for rulers everywhere. Dante Alighieri penned *Divine Comedy* in Italian. Soon native languages replaced classical languages like Latin and Greek. Martin Luther published the German translation of the Bible.

Did You Know?

A cultural movement called 'Humanism' during this period was a philosophy that all people should be educated in the classical arts, literature, and sciences.

Intellectual works during the Renaissance

This era witnessed new approaches to the various sciences, medicine and philosophy. Copernicus observed that Earth and other planets revolved around Sun. Renaissance medical scholars studied different body parts. Many universities were established during this period.

The Protestant Movement

During the sixteenth century, the Protestants rejected the authority of the Roman Catholic Church. Theirs was essentially a literary movement, as it stressed on an individual reading the works of the Bible rather than passively receiving sermons from the priests.

POCKET FACT

"The Renaissance" as it is known in French and, "Rinascimento" in Italian, was the after-effect of the growth of feudalism in places like Italy and Southern Holland.

Statue of Johannes Gutenberg

Discovery of the New World

The age of exploration started in the 1400s, with the European nations beginning to explore the world by travelling even further than the regular routes. It began by discovering new routes to India, then to the Far East, and finally, the Americas.

Christopher Columbus received by King Ferdinand and Queen Isabella on his return from the New World

Statue of Christopher Columbus

Christopher Columbus: The Explorer

Christopher Columbus wanted to find a sea route from Europe to Asia, but he made it across the other side and discovered America instead. On 3 August 1492, Columbus set sail from Palos and travelled for over two months. He set foot on the Caribbean islands of Bahamas and named the island San Salvador. He called the natives "Indians".

Map of Panama in Central America

Discovery of America

Italian explorer Amerigo Vespucci set sail for the land discovered by Columbus in search of gold, silver and spices. But he soon realised that he had not reached Asia but a new land. German map maker Martin Waldseemuller decided to call the new region "America" after Vespucci's first name.

Statue of Amerigo Vespucci at the Uffizi Loggia in Florence, Italy

The age of exploration

The job to assess the extent of Earth's expanse was first started by Ferdinand Magellan around 1519, but it was fully completed by Juan Sebastian around 1522. During these explorations, Europeans actually used the term "East Indies" for all of South East Asia, including India.

Ferdinand Magellan (1480–1521) was the first to start the expedition around the world

Did You Know?

Ferdinand Magellan gave the Pacific Ocean its name. After he sailed through bad weather and storms in South America, he entered the Strait of Magellan, which was a calmer ocean. Hence, he called it "Mar Pacifico", meaning Peaceful Sea in Portuguese.

Reformation

Reformation was a religious revolution that occurred during the sixteenth century, led by Martin Luther and John Calvin, among others. With the invention of the printing press, new ideas spread quickly and scriptures like the Bible were printed and distributed easily to people.

Martin Luther

The 95 Theses

A monk by the name of Martin Luther began to question the Catholic Church and its various practices. He published his writings as the 95 Theses in 1517. The 95 Theses stated that the Bible was the central authority and that people attained salvation through their faith, not their deeds. This was the basis for the Protestant Reformation.

Lutheran Church Dresden Frauenkirche in Dresden, German

King Henry VIII statue

Beginning of the Reformation Movement

Many new churches were established and were called the Lutheran Church and the Reformed Church. In Switzerland, John Calvin also spoke out against the Catholic Church's corrupt practices. King Henry VIII split from the Catholic Church. A few rulers converted to Protestantism, while some continued to support the Catholic Church. The religious divide led to the Thirty Years' War which involved most of Europe.

Counter Reformation

The Counter Reformation was the result of the efforts of the Roman Catholics against the Protestant Reformation. Pope Paul III requested for the prohibition of the luxurious living of the clergy. The Jesuits, known for their role in education, missionary work and theology, were founded in 1540 by St Ignatius of Loyola. Counter Reformation brought many people back to the Catholic Church in Austria, Poland, Holland, Germany and Hungary.

Reformation wall in Parc Des Bastions, Geneva, Switzerland. Sculptures of the four great figures of the Geneva protestant movement: Guillaume Farel, Jean Calvin, Theodore de Beze and John Knox

POCKET FACT

People started to feel that the Catholic Church's practices were inconsistent with the Bible's teachings and therein emerged a dissent, which transformed into a movement called the Protestant Reformation.

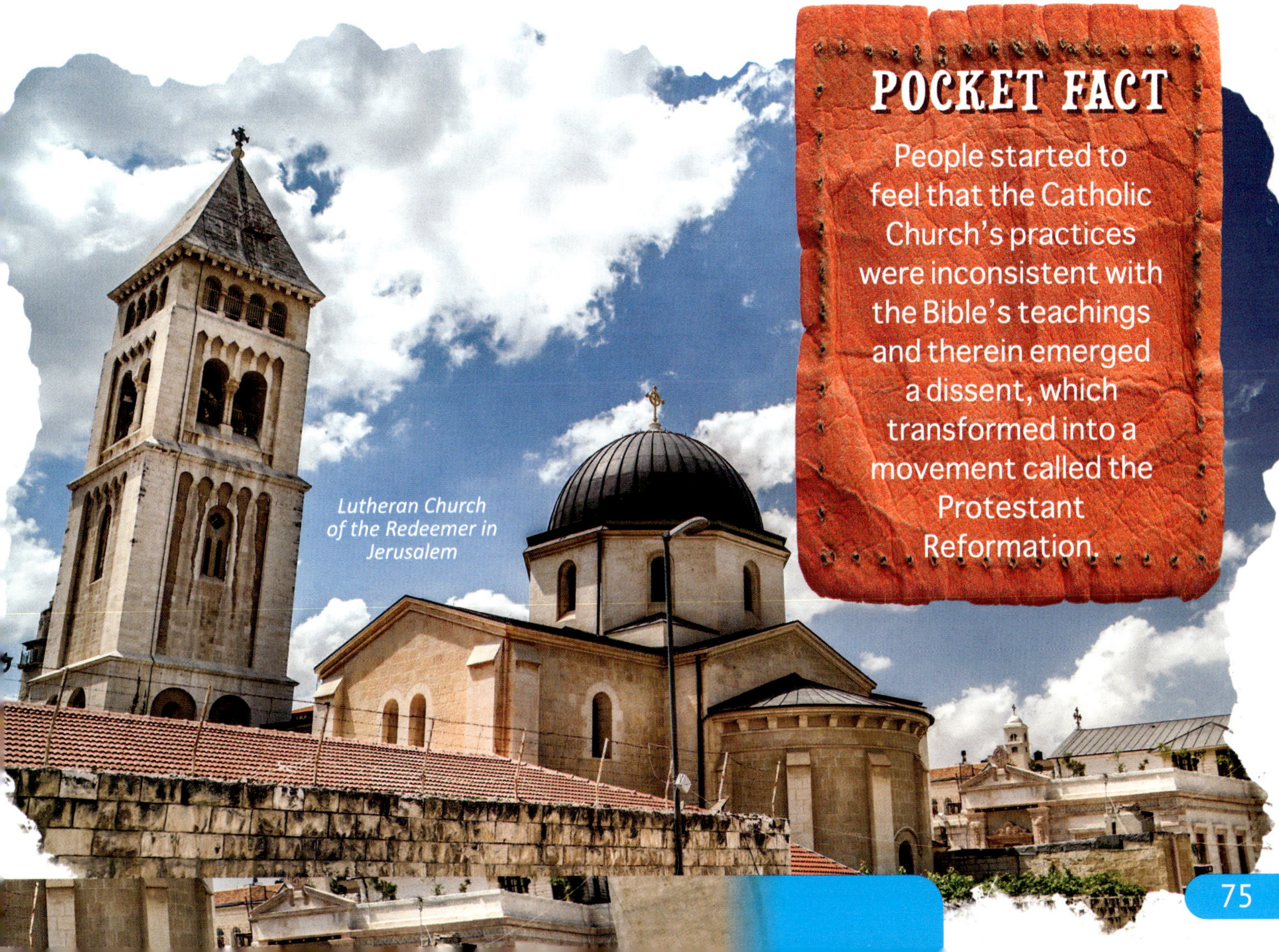

Lutheran Church of the Redeemer in Jerusalem

The Mughal Empire

The Mughal dynasty began their rule in Indian AD 1526. Under the Mughals, roads were built, trade prospered and the arts flourished. This glorious dynasty that ruled India for over 300 years, came to an end during the reign of Emperor Bahadur Shah.

Akbar the Great

The Mughal Dynasty

Babur, the first Mughal Emperor, was the descendent of Genghis Khan and Tamburlaine. He became a ruler at the age of 12. In 1526, he captured Delhi after ousting the forces of Ibrahim Lodhi in the first Battle of Panipat and defeated Rana Sanga of Mewar. Soon, Babur controlled a considerable portion of northern India.

Illustrations from the manuscript of Baburnama (Memoirs of Babur)—late 16th century

Tolerance policy

Babur's grandson Akbar expanded the empire and established an efficient administrative system. His son, Emperor Jahangir, followed his father's policy of religious tolerance. He was followed by Shah Jahan. The Taj Mahal and the Great Mosque of Delhi were built under his patronage.

Decline of the Empire

Emperor Shahjahan was succeeded by Aurangzeb. Aurangzeb did not follow the policy of religious tolerance. During his reign, he plundered and destroyed several temples and schools run or attended by other religions. This caused several rebellions to break out against him. Aurangzeb also levied heavy taxes on farmers who were already suffering. All these factors added to the slow decline of the Mughal Empire.

The advent of the British reduced the later Mughal rulers to mere puppets. Bahadur Shah II, the last Mughal emperor, was exiled to Yangon, Burma, by the British for his participation in the Indian Mutiny of 1857. This was the end of the Mughal Empire in India.

Emperor Aurangzeb

Did You Know?

According to historians, it was Babur who first brought gunpowder to India and used it extensively during wars.

Diorama of Battle of Panipat (1526) displayed at Indian War Memorial Museum, Naubat khana, India

Ottoman Empire

The Ottoman Empire was created by Turkish tribes and lasted for 600 years, ending in 1922. At its peak, the empire extended to three continents — stretching from the Balkans in southeastern Europe across Anatolia, Central Asia, Arabia, and North Africa.

Expansion of the Ottoman Empire

After the defeat of the Mongols in 1293, Osman became the prince of Byzantine Bithynia in North Western Anatolia. His successors focussed their attacks on territories near Bosporus and the Sea of Marmara. Mehmet II captured Constantinople, and converted it into his capital which is now called Istanbul.

Statues of an Ottoman Pasha and Janissary, Istanbul, Turkey

Suleiman the Magnificent also had a supreme army who were called "janissaries". The janissaries had unwavering faith and loyalty towards their Sultan and helped defeat King Louis of Hungary in the Battle of Mohacs in 1526.

Decline of the Empire

Suleiman began to spend more time devoted to pursuing the pleasures of life instead of focussing on the betterment of his people. The grand vizier did not have enough power or even the loyalty of all the Ottoman subjects, which brought about a lot of division within the empire itself. Internal corruption and poor leadership led to the decline of the Ottoman Empire until it was abolished and Turkey was declared a republic in 1923.

Battle of Mohacs, 1526
Askeri Military Museum in Istanbul, Turkey

POCKET FACT

The leader of the Ottoman Empire was known as the Sultan and the title was given to the eldest son. When the new Sultan took over the reign of the Empire, he would imprison his male siblings. When he had his own son, the Sultan would then kill his brothers. It was Ahmed I who put an end to this tradition of royal fratricide.

The Blue Mosque, constructed between 1609 and 1617 during the rule of Ahmed I, remains a functioning mosque today.

The Blue Mosque, Istanbul, Turkey

American Revolution

The American Revolution stands as a landmark moment in world history. It was an ideological and political revolution which occurred in colonial North America between 1765 and 1783, and resulted in the independence of the American colonies from the British rule.

Causes of the Revolution

Until the early 1760s, the British did not interfere much in the internal affairs of its American colonies. However, after the Seven Years' War, they began to exert more control over these colonies. The changing policies of their colonial rulers sparked widespread protests among the thirteen colonies. They together began to feel a growing desire for self-governance.

Boston Massacre

In March 1770, nine British soldiers shot several of a crowd of three or four hundred men in Boston who were harassing them verbally and throwing stones and sticks at them. This gave rise to revolutionary ideas, fuelled by Enlightenment philosophies, spread through pamphlets, newspapers, and public debates.

Road to Revolution

The First Continental Congress brought the colonial leaders together to discuss the grievances and explore peaceful solutions. However, the king disregarded their request for a fair treatment. Under the leadership of George Washington, the colonists organised the Continental Army to defend their rights and liberties.

POCKET FACT

Thomas Paine's influential pamphlet, "Common Sense," passionately argued for American independence from British rule.

Birth of a nation

The revolution faced numerous challenges, but the colonists finally won. The surrender of British forces in the decisive Battle of Yorktown made the path to independence clearer. The Treaty of Paris (1783) officially recognised the United States as an independent nation and ended the British colonial rule.

Treaty of Paris

Stars and Stripes

As the war drew to a close, there was need for a distinct national identity. The Stars and Stripes, the American flag, was adopted in 1777. It symbolised the unity and resolve of the newly formed United States. This iconic flag has since become a powerful representation of American values.

Prominent leaders of the Revolution

There were several prominent figures that played instrumental roles in shaping the course of the revolution. George Washington stands out as a central figure whose leadership, military prowess, resilience, and vision were critical to the success of the American Revolution.

Thomas Jefferson played an important role in drafting the Declaration of Independence. His articulation of the fundamental principles of equality, rights, and self-government laid the ideological foundation for the revolution. He also championed religious freedom and the separation of church and state.

Benjamin Franklin played a crucial role in securing vital foreign support for the American cause. His diplomatic efforts in France were instrumental in securing a critical alliance that provided military and financial assistance.

John Adams, a Massachusetts lawyer, was a vocal advocate for independence and played a significant role in shaping public opinion in favour of severing ties with Britain.

Did You Know?

The American Revolution was the United States' longest military conflict before the Vietnam War.

French Revolution

The French Revolution began in 1789 and ended in 1799. It was a time of social and political upheaval in France and its colonies. Years of feudal oppression and economic problems led to the French Revolution.

Reasons

The royal treasury was empty. For more than 20 years the country had suffered bad harvests. The rising inflation, imposition of heavy taxes, the exploitation of the peasants, and the extravagant life of the royalty— all together led to widespread frustration. The peasants wanted to end the feudal setup, and philosophers wanted to reform the political and social scene. This growing unrest among all quarters caused the great French Revolution.

A portrait of the Peasant War that called for the abolishment of the feudal system

Formation of a new constitution

On 26 August 1789, the Declaration of the Rights of Man and of the Citizen was introduced, which claimed liberty, equality, inviolability of property and the right to resist oppression. It was committed to the replacement of the ancient regime with one that focussed on equal opportunity, freedom of speech, sovereignty, and, most importantly, a representative government.

The motto of French Revolution

POCKET FACT

The guillotine was a popular method of punishment during the French Revolution. It remained a legal form of execution in France right up till 1981.

Reign of Terror

Louis XVI was executed for treason in January 1793. Maximilien de Robespierre took over. The fear of counter-revolutionary forces made him start a Reign of Terror. From 1793 to 1794, he executed more than 15,000 people at the guillotine for being alleged enemies of the revolution.

Napoleon Bonaparte

Napoleon Bonaparte, also known as the "Little Corporal", was an important personality in the national history of France. He became the French general, first consul and also the emperor of the French.

Napoleon becomes a national hero

While fighting against Austria in 1796, Napoleon took over the command of the French army. He was an efficient leader, and soon the Austrians were forced to leave Italy. When the victory was announced back home, Napoleon was hailed as a national hero. In 1802, Napoleon proclaimed himself "First Consul for Life".

Napoleon the leader

Napoleon demonstrated great prowess in restoring peace and order after the French Revolution. He had worked very hard to gain the support of the Royalist faction. Napoleon even announced Catholicism as the official religion of the Republic of France to improve relations with the Catholic Church.

Napoleon crossing the Alps

The Napoleonic Code

Under this, all male citizens were perceived to be equal whether rich or poor. The previous French traditions of class over mass, privileges to the rich and hereditary nobility were removed.

The Napoleonic Era

Napoleon crowned himself the emperor of France in May 1804. He wanted to establish a French-dominated empire in Europe. He won many battles for France. He would collect tax from the territories he conquered in other nations and used the money to repair France's failing economy.

Louisiana state quarter coin and old French coins used in 1856

The Napoleonic Code in Speyer, Historical Museum of the Palatinate

Napoleon abdicates

During the Peninsular War, Napoleon's army lost many battles at the same time against Prussia, Britain, Russia, Sweden and Austria. Finally, he was forced to abdicate. On 6 April 1814 Napoleon was exiled to Elba, a Mediterranean island. However, Napoleon escaped to Paris, where he mobilised a new army and again engaged in a series of battles. In the Battle of Waterloo, Napoleon was defeated and forced to abdicate once again. This brought the Napoleonic Era to an end.

The Battle of Marengo (14 June 1800) helped bring the French Revolutionary Wars to an end and consolidated Bonaparte's new position as First Consul of the French Republic.

Battle of Marengo

Industrial Revolution

The Industrial Revolution was also a time of invention.

The Industrial Revolution took place in Europe between the eighteenth and nineteenth centuries. From Britain, this revolution spread to Europe and North America, and then to the rest of the world.

Reasons

The use of iron and steel as raw materials, the discovery of coal and improved transportation, such as with the steam engine, kick-started the industrialisation of Europe. New machines enabled the mass production of goods.

Change from agriculture to industry

At the beginning of the revolution, the European nations practised agriculture. All nations had predominantly rural societies. It was during this revolution that urban and industrial practices were developed.

A steam engine with the intricate parts

Technological change

The factory system came into existence. The means of communication improved with the introduction of the radio and telegraph. The textile industry improved with inventions like the spinning jenny by James Hargreaves. James Watt enhanced the efficiency of steam engines.

Did You Know?

A historian named Arnold Toynbee first used the term "Industrial Revolution" to show England's economic development.

POCKET FACT

The spinning of cotton into thread on a spinning wheel was the first thing that launched England into the Industrial Revolution.

Migration to cities

Rural workers started moving towards cities to get jobs in factories. The population increased and cities expanded. The cost of labour for factories became cheap.

Employment of cheap labour

Machines were doing everything, so factories employed unskilled workers. Most factories had 15-hour working days. These conditions led to many people falling sick or dying.

Change in gender roles

Prior to the Industrial Revolution, both men and women worked together in cottage industries. The roles of men and women began to change as women entered factories as workers.

Transformation of transportation

The Industrial Revolution saw stronger roads, the building of canals and the introduction of railway lines. Raw materials were now transported using faster means.

Advance of Democracy

Even though democracy was gaining collective support in England, Prime Minister Arthur Wellesley opposed parliamentary reforms in 1830. However, when the new government under Earl Grey came into power, England saw parliamentary reforms that supported democracy.

Women suffrage in Wyoming Territory–women voting at the polls in Cheyenne, Wyoming, 24 November 1888

Democracy

Democracy is a system of government in which state power is vested in the people, who vote their elected representatives into parliament.

Representation of the People Act of 1832

Prime Minister Earl Grey had promised parliamentary reforms when he rose to power. He managed to get the royal assent at the third attempt in the passing of the reform bills in 1832. The bills proposed the first changes to electoral franchise legislation in more than 50 years. William IV needed to support them for the bills to be passed.

The Wellington Monument in Hyde Park, was built in honour of the first Duke of Wellington, Arthur Wellesley, and his triumph in the Peninsular and Napoleonic wars.

Creation of new constituencies

The Reform Act of 1832 (also known as the Representation of the People Act of 1832) created 67 new constituencies, including small owners of land, farmers and shopkeepers. This increased the size of the electorate from a mere 435,000 to 652,000.

Empowerment of the middle class

The Act formed a uniform franchise in the boroughs. It also provided voting rights to the middle class. All householders who paid a rental of more than ten pounds now had the right to vote. This granting of voting rights enabled the middle class to have some amount of influence in politics. However, these were limited efforts. Many from the labour force could not vote.

The Reform Act of 1867

The Reform Act of 1867 further modernised the franchise and the electoral system. It even managed to give voting rights to the labour forces in cities.

The American Civil War

The American Civil War, fought from 1861 to 1865, stands as one of the most pivotal and defining moments in the history of the United States. The conflict tested the very foundation of the United States.

The two sides

The Civil War pitted two distinct regions of the United States against each other: the Union, primarily composed of northern states, and the Confederacy, comprising the southern states. This brutal conflict between the North and the South tore the nation apart as ideological, economic, and political differences escalated into a devastating struggle.

The differences

The underlying cause of the war was the stark contrast in economic systems and social structures between the industrialised North and the agrarian South. While the North embraced modernisation and an evolving society, the South held onto a plantation-based economy reliant on slave labour.

Slaves during the war

The Civil War marked a turning point for enslaved African Americans. As the conflict raged on, many slaves escaped to Union lines, seeking freedom from the shackles of bondage. Their actions had a profound impact on the course of the war, as their labour and support contributed to the Union's war effort.

End of the war

The war finally came to an end in April 1865. The Confederacy collapsed, and there began the Reconstruction era, a period of rebuilding and reform in the South. Slavery was abolished throughout the United States. Thus, the war brought profound changes to society, politics, and the nation's understanding of liberty and equality.

Did You Know?

President Abraham Lincoln's role during the Civil War was of paramount importance. He was an advocate of the Union and the abolition of the institution of slavery.

Abraham Lincoln

Abraham Lincoln, the 16th President of the United States, is one of the most iconic figures in American history. He played a crucial role in preserving the Union and abolishing slavery during the American Civil War.

Early life and political career

Abraham Lincoln was born on 12 February 1809, in a log cabin in Hardin County, Kentucky. His early life experiences instilled in him a strong work ethic and a deep sense of empathy for the common people.

Lincoln's Election as the President

Lincoln was elected President of the United States in 1860. His stance against the expansion of slavery in new territories fuelled tensions between the North and South. As Southern states declared their separation and formed the Confederate States of America, Lincoln faced the monumental challenge of preserving the Union.

Leadership during the Civil War

President Abraham Lincoln's role during the Civil War was of paramount importance. A skilled orator and pragmatic leader, Lincoln was committed to preserving the Union and ending the institution of slavery. His exceptional qualities as a leader, his political acumen, and his unwavering commitment to the principles of freedom and equality have made him an enduring symbol of leadership during times of crisis.

Emancipation Proclamation

Lincoln's Emancipation Proclamation in 1863 declared that all slaves in the Confederate territory were to be set free, transforming the war from a conflict over secession to a moral struggle for human rights.

POCKET FACT

Lincoln's Gettysburg Address of 1863 reinforced the ideals of equality and democracy enshrined in the Declaration of Independence.

Legacy and impact

Lincoln's leadership and steadfast determination helped guide the Union through the darkest days of the war. His legacy endures as a testament to the power of leadership to shape history and create a more just and united society.

World War I (1914-1918)

The First World War resulted from the increasing tension in the Balkan regions. Amidst the disputes, came the assassination of Franz Ferdinand, the archduke of Austria-Hungary, by a Serbian nationalist. This propelled European powers towards the Great War.

The beginning

The Balkan regions had been witnessing severe disputes after the two Balkan Wars. The Serbian and Austrian tension had not yet subsided, when Franz Ferdinand, heir apparent to the throne of Austria-Hungary, was assassinated. On 29 July, Austro-Hungarian military started bombarding Belgrade. Germany wanted Russia and France to take a neutral stand in the war. When Russia and France ignored the request, Germany declared war against them.

French military helmets of World War I

Troops ride on World War I tanks going forward to the battle line in the Forest of Argonne, France

Technological weapons

With World War I, the world was able to witness the destructive side of technology. Nations fell and new nations were born. German troops used machine guns, fortifications, trenches, poisonous gases and barbed wires. Submarines or German U-boats attacked ships with torpedoes. Fighter aircrafts with machine guns and planned bombings were initiated.

Rest of the world joins the war

The US had joined the Allied Forces (France, the United Kingdom, Russia, Italy, and Japan) and made financial contributions in purchasing armaments and supplies. It sent food to the nations and armies of the Allies. Soon, Japan and China also joined the war. Both sided with the Allies.

The Allies emerge victorious

The Allied powers won the war. Germany signed a peace treaty with Russia. It deployed its forces on its western border. But the allied troops pushed the Germans back. Germany had to withdraw its forces from all the territories it had occupied. It had to give up its weapons including airplanes, submarines and battleships.

Destruction caused by the war

World War I caused massive devastation. It is estimated that eight million soldiers and nine million civilians died. The war also destroyed thousands of houses, factories, railway lines and coal mines. This war brought Germany towards the brink of an economic collapse.

The war upset the European economies. USA became the chief creditor and industrial power.

Treaty of Versailles

The Treaty of Versailles was a peace document signed at the end of World War I between the Allied powers and Germany in the Palace of Versailles, France, on 28 June 1919. The Treaty of Versailles ended the state of war between Germany and most of the Allied Powers. The primary purpose of the treaty was to establish the terms of peace and address the aftermath of the war. It aimed at preventing future conflicts.

According to the treaty, limitations were imposed on the German army and its naval fleet, and it was prohibited from keeping an air force. Germany was forced to accept full responsibility for causing the war and pay compensation to the Allies.

Did You Know?

During World War I, many soldiers suffered shrapnel wounds to the face. Harold Gillies, a pioneer in the field of plastic surgery made dedicated attempts to improve and develop the procedure of facial reconstruction.

League of Nations

The League of Nations was established in 1920 as a part of the Treaty of Versailles. It was like a precursor to the modern United Nations. Its main goals were to promote global peace and cooperation, prevent aggression, and facilitate peaceful resolution of international disputes through diplomatic negotiations.

Luxemburg women wave Allied flags from their windows to greet the Occupation of the American Army at the end of World War I

The Russian Revolution

The Russian Revolution was a movement started by the Bolshevik Party of Russia in the year 1917. This revolution aimed to end the Tsarist system followed in Russia and led to the formation of the Soviet Union.

Formation of a new republic

There was widespread discontent with the autocratic rule of Tsar Nicholas II and the hardships faced by the Russian people due to the strain of World War I. Demonstrations and strikes in Petrograd culminated in the overthrow of the tsarist regime. Nicholas II abdicated the throne, and a provisional government, consisting mainly of liberal and moderate socialist factions, was established.

Military help

The Bolsheviks were discontent with the provisional government's inability to address pressing issues such as land reform, food shortages, and the continuation of the war. Besides, there was a growing support for socialist ideals. This led to a coup by the Bolsheviks. They seized key government buildings in Petrograd, including the Winter Palace, and effectively took control of the country.

Bolshevik parade in St Petersberg during the Russian Revolution in the spring of 1917

The Bolsheviks, under the leadership of Vladimir Lenin, established a socialist government and transformed Russia into the Russian Soviet Federative Socialist Republic (RSFSR), laying the groundwork for the formation of the Union of Soviet Socialist Republics (USSR) in 1922.

Bolshevik Revolution, 1917

World War II (1939-1945)

An old hand grenade and bullet

After World War I, Germany, Italy, and Japan witnessed a rise of authoritarian, military regimes. These states were also eager to regain power. All this, coupled with the failure of the League of Nations, gradually led the world towards the Second World War.

Adolf Hitler in Nuremberg to attend a Nazi Party Convention in September 1934

Nazi award - Knight's Cross of the Iron Cross

The Knight's Cross of the Iron Cross or simply the Knight's Cross and its variants, were the highest awards in the military and paramilitary forces of Nazi Germany during World War II.

Events leading to the war

World War II was fought between the Axis Powers comprising Germany, Italy, Japan and the Allied Powers comprising Britain, USA, Soviet Union and France. Adolf Hitler took over the reins of Germany by 1933. Hitler wanted to invade and occupy Poland which had the support of France and Britain. Germany attacked Poland in 1939. Britain and France responded by declaring war on Germany and this sparked off World War II.

Weaponry used in the war

Vintage American M24 Tank

World War II was the largest armed war in human history. A larger number of countries were involved in World War II than in World War I. Several significant scientific developments impacted the use of weaponry in the war. Dive bombers, monoplane fighter planes, machine guns, light and medium bombers were some of the weapons employed in air warfare during World War II. Nuclear weapons were used in warfare for the first time during this war.

Hitler and World War II

Adolf Hitler played a very crucial role in the Second World War right from the start. His military ambition led to the war. In addition, he planned a series of invasions, which were strategically very important for Germany. By 1941, Hitler's troops had occupied much of Europe and North Africa. Hitler established concentration camps to imprison Jews, leading to the death of more than six million people in the Holocaust.

POCKET FACT

Despite being the person responsible for building concentration camps that imprisoned Jews, Hitler never visited a concentration camp in his lifetime.

Italy joins the war

Hitler had for long been inspired by the Italian dictator, Mussolini's, achievements. In 1936, Hitler secured Mussolini's partnership, and Italy joined the war against the Allies. The two leaders of Germany and Italy signed a complete defence alliance with Germany, known as the Pact of Steel.

Battle of Britain

The Battle of Britain began on 10 July 1940 with Germany bombing England. Britain put up a good defence. When the German troops began to feel that they were very close to conquering England, the RAF shot down many German planes. The war lasted for three months.

USA joins the war

Although the USA did not get directly involved in the war at its advent, it sought ways to help the European states constantly. The 1941 Japanese bombing of the US Pacific fleet at Pearl Harbour pulled USA into World War II. The Allied powers now fought back with renewed force. The Battle of Normandy in 1944 led to the freedom of Western Europe from Germany's control.

The fall of Mussolini

Italy suffered many military defeats during World War II. By 1943, The opposition groups in Italy came together to overthrow Mussolini and make peace with the Allies, but the German army stopped such an act. However, soon Italy was severely defeated and the Allied forces captured Sicily. As a result, Mussolini was deposed in a coup. He tried to cross the frontier disguised as a German soldier, but he was recognised, shot and killed on 28 April 1945.

Benito Mussolini met with a series of defeats between 1940-43

The European World War ends

Germany found itself caught up between the Soviet troops and the advancing Western Allies. The Western Allies crossed the Rhine River and moved eastward toward Berlin. Seeing that defeat was inevitable, Hitler committed suicide in his bunker on 30 April 1945. Consequently, the German forces surrendered. By midnight of 8 May 1945, the war in Europe was formally over.

Did You Know?

An American B-29 bomber dropped the first atomic bomb over the Japanese city of Hiroshima. It destroyed around 90 per cent of the city and killed 80,000 people. Three days later, the second bomb was dropped on Nagasaki, killing around 40,000 people.

Soviet aircraft of World War II

Surrender of Japan

The US dropped atomic bombs on the Japanese cities of Hiroshima and Nagasaki in August 1945. Japan's Emperor Hirohito decided that his country must surrender. At noon on August 15 the Emperor announced Japan's formal surrender, which was accepted. This brought an end to the Second World War.

Operation Torch plaque

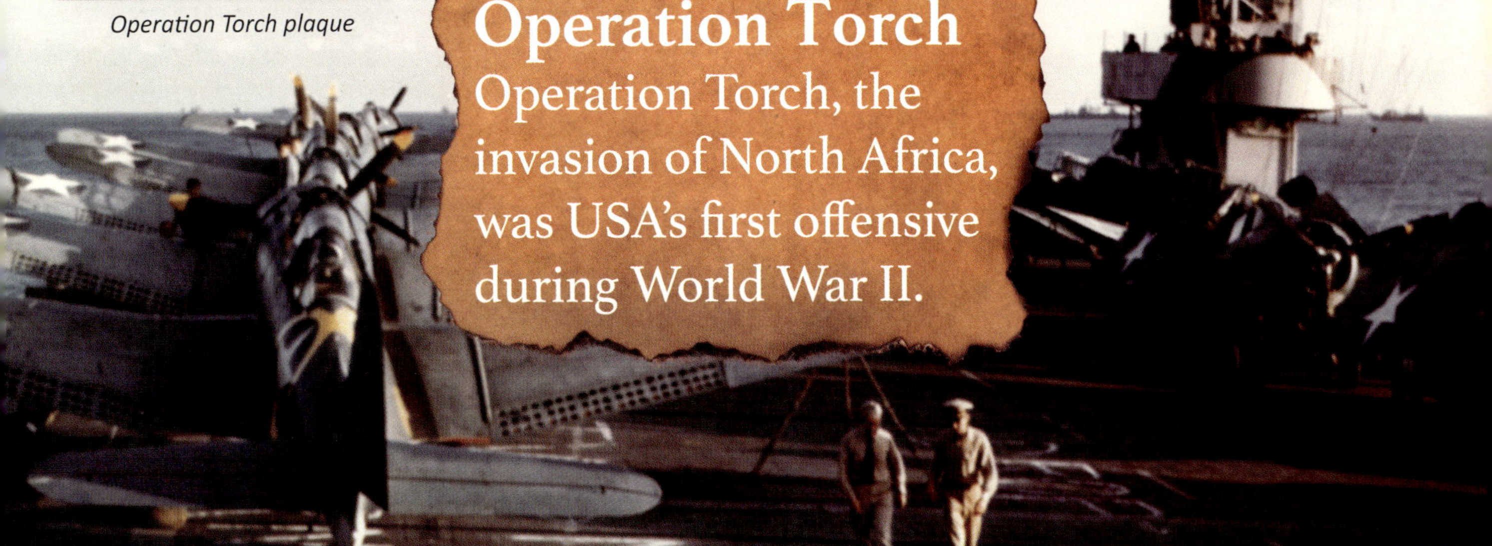

Operation Torch

Operation Torch, the invasion of North Africa, was USA's first offensive during World War II.

United Nations Organisation

The formation of the United Nations Organisation (UNO) marked a significant step towards global peace and cooperation. It was a direct response to the devastation caused by World War II and aimed to prevent such global conflicts in the future.

Background

World War II was one of the most devastating conflicts in human history. It resulted in a massive loss of life, widespread destruction, and significant socio-economic upheaval. The League of Nations failed to prevent the outbreak of war and could not effectively address the post-war challenges.

Steps towards the formation

The need of the hour was to establish a more powerful world order to promote peace, security, international cooperation, and the protection of human rights.

Representatives from the United States, the United Kingdom, the Soviet Union, and China met at several conferences to lay the groundwork for the formation of a new international organisation. They discussed the framework, the structure and the objectives of the future international organisation.

Formation of the United Nations

On 26 June 1945, representatives from 50 nations signed the United Nations Charter, officially establishing the United Nations Organisation. The charter came into effect on 24 October 1945, now celebrated as United Nations Day. Thus, the League of Nations was eventually replaced by the United Nations after World War II.

Key Objectives of the UN

- Maintenance of international. peace and security.
- Protecting and promoting. human rights.
- Improving living conditions. and fostering sustainable. development around the world.
- Providing aid and assistance to countries affected by natural disasters, conflicts, and other emergencies.

Agencies of the UN

The United Nations consists of various bodies—General Assembly, Security Council, International Court of Justice, World Health Organisation (WHO), United Nations Educational, Scientific and Cultural Organisation (UNESCO), etc.

Over the decades, the UN has played a central role in addressing global challenges, promoting human rights, and facilitating international cooperation across a wide range of issues.

British Rule

In 1858, British Crown rule was established in India, thus, ending more than 100 years of control under the East India Company. This changed the structure of the political, social and economic rule that the British had established.

Old illustration of British soldiers battling insurgents near Delhi

After effects of the Mutiny of 1857

The Indian Mutiny or "First War of Indian Independence" had far-reaching impacts on the country despite its failure. The East India Company was abolished. The Mughal Empire also came to an end and soon Queen Victoria was announced as the ruler of India. Thus, India came directly under the British Rule. The rise of nationalism had made the British understand that they would now have to work towards some amount of development of the country.

Queen Victoria

Growing racial gulf between Indians and the British rulers

The Mutiny of 1857 created a racial gap between the Indians and the British. This continued until the end of the British Raj.

E M Forster and Rudyard Kipling reflected this amply in their works. The British Empire appointed viceroys who had little knowledge about India and its people.

Economic benefits from India

Britain's main objective of being in India was because it made for a great economic investment. The British invested in infrastructure and built the railways network. They also built canals and other irrigation works and established the English education system. India also offered a good market for goods and services.

POCKET FACT

E. M. Forster's, "A Passage to India" has good insights into the racial and social isolation towards native Indians, practised by the British that continued right till the end of British Raj.

Steam engine

Rise of industrialisation

The first cotton textile mill was set up in 1853 in Bombay by Cowasjee Nanabhoy. Soon, the first jute mill was established in 1855 in Bengal. A majority of the modern Indian industries were controlled by the British.

picture of old textile mill

Formation of Indian National Congress

The delegates to the first meeting of the Indian National Congress in Bombay, 1885

According to Lord Dufferin, the Viceroy of India, Indian intellectuals needed to have a collective forum to forward the grievances of Indians before the British government. So, the Indian National Congress was formed in 1885 to fight for India's independence from Britain.

Indian National Union

Mr Allan Octavian Hume, a retired member of Indian Civil Service, helped establish the collective organisation and named it Indian National Union. The first session of the Indian National Union was held on 28-30 December 1885, and was presided over by W C Banerjee, A O Hume, K T Telang, Subramanya Aiyar and Dadabhai Naoroji.

A O Hume, Dadabhai Naroji and Wedderburn meeting at the Indian National Congress

The grand old man of India, Dadabhai Naroji

Aim of the Indian National Congress

The primary aim of the Indian National Congress was to simply put in place a base towards the creation of a secular and democratic national movement. It worked towards making the people politically aware, to put in place a headquarters for this and to ensure that it becomes an all-India leadership entity that could organically help create an anti-British strategy.

Mahatma Gandhi discussing the "Quit India" movement with Nehru, 1942

Boycott of British goods

By the early twentieth century, the Congress began the "swadeshi" movement. This movement urged people to boycott all British goods and encouraged them to use goods that were produced indigenously.

Move towards self-rule

British social reformer Annie Besant and Indian nationalist Bal Gangadhar Tilak started the Home Rule wing in 1917. This was known as the extremist wing of the Indian National Congress.

Did You Know

Dadabhai, also known as the grand old man of India, suggested that the Indian National Union be re-named as Indian National Congress.

Mahatma Gandhi became a global symbol of peace due to his peaceful method of solving disputes of which one was the boycott of British goods.

Jallianwala Bagh Massacre

On 13 April 1919, Amritsar's Jallianwala Bagh witnessed the merciless killing by the British of several hundred civilians, including men, women and children. Hundreds more people were wounded.

Close-up of a bullet mark from the massacre at Jallianwala Bagh

Before the massacre

In protest to the Rowlatt Act, Amritsar had observed a peace hartal on 30 March and 6 April 1919 and the British government wanted to repress the protest. On 10 April Dr Satyapala and Dr Kitchlew, two popular leaders of the province, were deported from Amritsar.

The massacre

On Baisakhi day, Sunday 13 April 1919, tens of thousands of unarmed men, women and children gathered at Amritsar's Jallianwala Bagh to attend a protest meeting, despite a ban on public meetings. General Dyer reached the place with British Indian Army soldiers. He ordered his soldiers to fire into the gathering. There was no warning issued to disperse the crowds.

Jallianwala Bagh memorial in Amritsar, Punjab, India

For about 15 minutes, 1,650 rounds of ammunition were unloaded into the screaming, terrified crowd. Jallianwala Bagh was closed on all sides by houses and buildings and there were just a few narrow entrances, which were generally locked. The main entrance was a bit wide, but was secured by British troops.

Events of the massacre

During the shooting, a number of people died in the stampede in their attempt to get away from the Bagh, but got caught at the narrow gates. A few jumped into the solitary well to escape the shooting. The wounded could not be shifted when the curfew was declared, adding to the casualties.

Effect of the massacre

The massacre instigated and fuelled nationalist feelings across Indians and had a deep impact on the leaders of the freedom struggle. It propelled Gandhi to start off India's first civil resistance movement called the Non-cooperation Movement also called Rowlett Satyagraha against Britain's tyrannical rule.

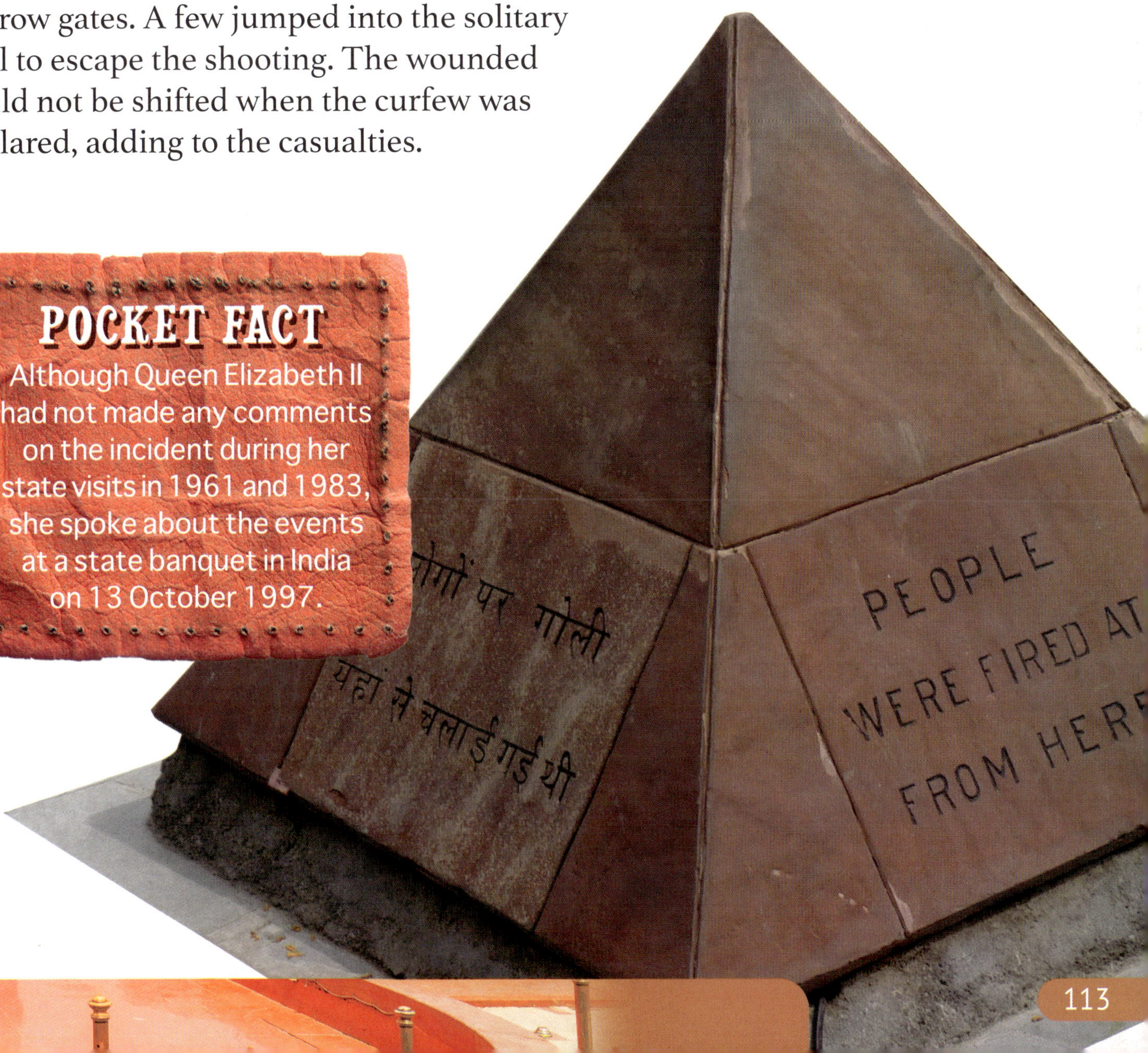

POCKET FACT

Although Queen Elizabeth II had not made any comments on the incident during her state visits in 1961 and 1983, she spoke about the events at a state banquet in India on 13 October 1997.

Pre-Independence Movements

Beginning 1920s, the Congress endorsed a series of non-violent, non-cooperation campaigns against the British rule under the leadership of Gandhi.

Gandhi and Sardar Patel, Bardoli Satyagraha, 1928

Non-cooperation Movement

The Non-cooperation movement was launched in 1920. The movement urged people to resign titles, boycott government educational institutions, courts, government services, foreign goods, elections, refuse to pay taxes and to use the charkha and khadi. Muslim leaders formed the Khilafat Committee to fight the British.

Civil Disobedience Movement

The Indian National Congress led the nationwide Civil Disobedience Movement and advocated for the revocation of the tax levied by the British. This movement began in 1930 with the Dandi March. Gandhi marched with his followers to protest against the taxes levied on salt. People all over the country boycotted British goods and services. Peasants started refusing to pay taxes.

A spinning wheel which became the symbol of the boycott of foreign cloth

POCKET FACT

Gandhi began the Salt March with a mere 78 followers, but this number grew to tens of thousands by the time he reached Dandi.

Discussing the "Quit India" movement with Nehru, 1942

Role of Indian National Army (INA)

Azad Hind Fauj or the Indian National Army was first established by Mohan Singh in 1942. It comprised Indian prisoners of war trained by Mohan Singh. INA was later revived by Netaji Subhas Chandra Bose on 21 October 1943 during the Second World War to secure India's complete independence from British Raj.

Quit India Movement

The Quit India Movement was launched in 1942. It called for a mass non-violent protest. The British declared the movement and the INC illegal. Intense non-violent resistance resulted in the imprisonment of most of the Congress leaders like Maulana Abul Kalam Azad, Netaji Subhash Chandra Bose, Mahatma Gandhi, Muhammad Ali Jinnah, Asoka Mehta, Jaya Prakash Narayan, Jawaharlal Nehru, and Chakravarti Rajgopalachari. The Quit India Movement showed the British that their time as the rulers of India was at its end.

Did You Know?

The Quit India Movement had three phases. The first phase involved processions and strikes. The second phase involved raiding government buildings. The third phase saw mobs retaliating against the police.

Netaji Subhash Chandra Bose

Salt march statue

India Gains Independence

In February 1947, Britain announced that India would be granted freedom by June 1948. Finally, at midnight on 14 August 1947, India was declared an independent nation.

Overcrowded train transferring refugees during tl partition of India, 1947

Fixing of the border

The partition issue was largely debated and strongly opposed at first. Indian Viceroy Lord Louis Mountbatten asked for a unified India and requested the Hindus and Muslims to agree to the formation of such a country. Unfortunately, with violence erupting across the country, Mountbatten agreed to form two separate states and changed the date for granting independence to 15 August 1947.

Once it was clear that the partition would be carried out, the task of fixing a border between the new states assumed grave importance. The interests of not only the Hindus and Muslims but also of the Sikhs, Christians and other religions were taken into consideration. Finally, it was decided that the border for the two states would be made between Lahore and Amritsar.

Lord Mountbatten

The Partition

This Partition was highly controversial and not without blood; more than 500,000 on both sides lost their lives. Millions of people fled from either side to avoid the violence that came with the partition. Thousands of women were abducted. Cities were swarming with refugees crossing borders.

The birth of two nations

At 11:57 p.m. on 14 August 1947, Pakistan was declared a separate nation. A new country was formed. Even today, this day is celebrated as Independence Day in Pakistan.

Did You Know?

On 30 January 1948, Gandhiji was shot by Nathuram Godse because of his acceptance to create a multi-religious state.

About five minutes later, at 12:02 a.m., India was granted her freedom. It was a memorable moment that came after over an almost 100-year-long struggle for freedom against the British rule. It took many rebellions and the sacrifice of many brave lives, but India was finally a free nation.

Gandhi assassinated

Freedom at Midnight

Jawaharlal Nehru gives his speech

Pt Jawaharlal Nehru became the first Prime Minister of independent India. He delivered the speech on "Tryst with Destiny" in the Indian Constituent Assembly on the eve of India's Independence during midnight on 14 August 1947.

People celebrating indian independence in 1947

Dr. Rajendra Prasad

C. Rajagopachari

Vallabh Bhai Patel

Excerpts of Nehru's historic speech

Before the birth of freedom, we have endured all the pains of labour and our hearts are heavy with the memory of this sorrow. Some of those pains continue even now. Nevertheless, the past is over and it is the future that beckons to us now. That future is not one of ease or resting, but of incessant striving so that we might fulfil the pledges we have so often taken and the one we shall take today. The service of India means the service of the millions who suffer. It means the ending of poverty and ignorance and disease and inequality of opportunity.

The future beckons to us. Whither do we go and what shall be our endeavour? To bring freedom and opportunity to the common man, to the peasants and workers of India; to fight and end poverty and ignorance and disease; to build up a prosperous, democratic and progressive nation, and to create social, economic and political institutions, which will ensure justice and fullness of life to every man and woman.

We have hard work ahead. There is no resting for any one of us till we redeem our pledge in full, till we make all the people of India what destiny intended them to be.

We are citizens of a great country, on the verge of bold advance, and we have to live up to that high standard. All of us, to whatever religion we may belong, are equally the children of India with equal rights, privileges and obligations. We cannot encourage communalism or narrow-mindedness, for no nation can be great whose people are narrow in thought or in action. To the nations and peoples of the world, we send greetings and pledge ourselves to co-operate with them in furthering peace, freedom and democracy. And to India, our much-loved motherland, the ancient, the eternal and the ever-new, we pay our reverent homage and we bind ourselves afresh to her service. Jai Hind.

Other leaders of Independent India

Sardar Vallabhbhai Patel was appointed the Deputy Prime Minister. He, together with Pt Nehru, focussed on uniting the princely states as a part of India. Lord Mountbatten was invited to continue as the Governor General of India, but he was replaced in the following year by Chakravarti Rajagopalachari. While the country was celebrating its independence, work had already begun on the drafting of its new constitution. This was done by 26 January 1950 and the Republic of India was officially proclaimed. Dr Rajendra Prasad was elected as the first President of India.

POCKET FACT

India awoke to freedom at midnight hour and the Constituent Assembly began its sitting at 11 p.m. with the singing of Vande Mataram by Sucheta Kripalani.

Fun Facts

1 Both Egyptian men and women wore make-up. The eye paint was usually green (made from copper) or black (made from lead)to protect from the sun. The Egyptians also believed that make-up had magical healing powers.

2 The Germans and British soldiers stopped fighting the war for a day on Christmas Day 1914. They sang, drank and celebrated together and played football.

3 Adolf Hitler's nephew William Patrick Hitler served in the US Navy and fought against the Nazis in World War II.

4 Ancient Egyptians used crescent-shaped stone pillows to support the neck. The pillow protected against worms and insects from getting into the nose, ears, and eyes since people slept on the ground.

5 The Mayans worshipped turkeys as gods.

6 America's 16th President Abraham Lincoln's wrestling abilities were formally recognised by the National Wrestling Hall of Fame. A mural of Lincoln engaged in a wrestling match adorns the wall just inside the front doors of the Hall of Fame museum in Oklahoma.

7 Once in 1807, during a rabbit hunt, the bunnies retaliated and charged straight towards Napoleon. They climbed up his legs and nibbled at his buttons. They attacked on either side of Napoleon who ran to his carriage.

8 India is a peace-loving country. It has never invaded any country in the last thousands of years.

Let's Recall

Choose the correct answer.

1. Which is the best known earliest human species?
   (a) Homo sapien
   (b) Australopithecus afarensis
   (c) Homo neanderthalensis
   (d) Australopithecus africanus

2. The Mesolithic Age was also known as the ______________.

   (a) The Iron Age
   (b) The New Stone Age
   (c) The Old Stone Age
   (d) The Middle Stone Age

3. Why were dogs tamed by the early settlers?
   (a) for farming
   (b) for hunting and guarding against wild animals
   (c) for meat
   (d) for milk

4. Which of these leaders drafted the American Declaration of Independence?
   (a) Thomas Jefferson (b) Benjamin Franklin
   (c) John Adams (d) George Washington

5. Magna Carta was signed between
   (a) Hitler and Mussolini
   (b) William the Conqueror and the barons of England
   (c) King John and the barons of England
   (d) France and Austria

Answers: 1. (b) Australopithecus afarensis 2. (d) The Middle Stone Age
3. (b) For hunting and guarding against wild animals
4. (a) Thomas Jefferson 5. (c) King John and the barons of England

Read the following statements and say whether they are true or false.

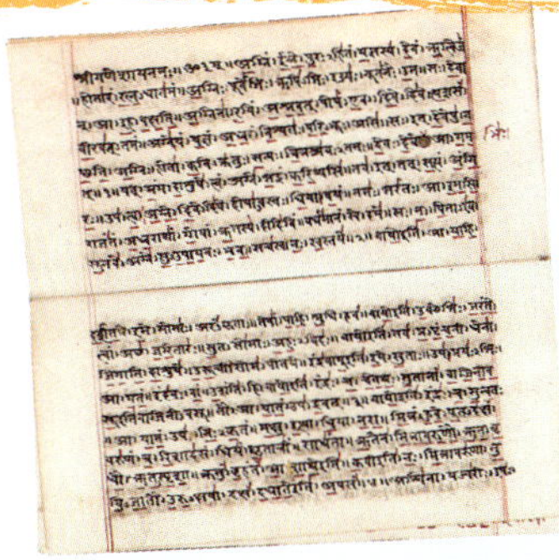

1. Rig Veda was written during the Prehistoric Period.

2. The period of Dinosaurs was called the Ice Age.

3. Civil Disobedience Movement started with the Dandi March.

4. The mammoths walked the Earth during the Jurassic Age.

5. Napoleon Bonaparte was also known as 'Little Corporal'.

Answers: 1. False 2. False 3. True 4. False 5. True

Match the given descriptions with the pictures.

1. The first Prime Minister of India

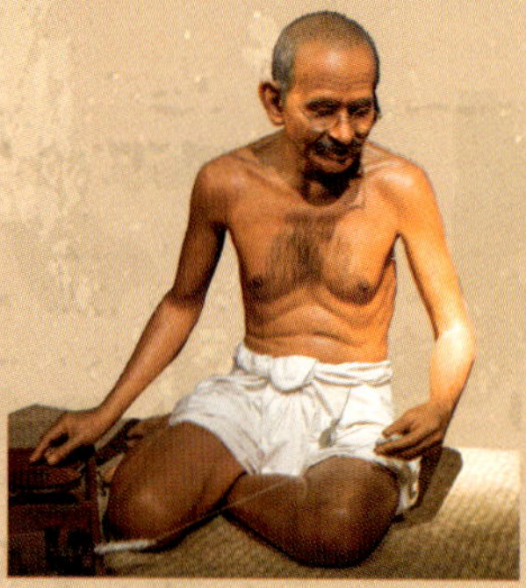

2. The champion of the American Civil War

3. A German dictator

4. He started the Civil Disobedience Movement

5. The Father of History

Answers: 1. Jawaharlal Nehru 2. Abraham Lincoln 3. Mahatma Gandhi 4. Adolf Hitler 5. Herodotus

Give the correct answer.

1. What do you call a person who studies and writes history?

2. Give another name for the Neolithic Age.

3. Which was the largest city state in Greece?

4. Who wore Togas as a national costume?

5. Name the first movable printing press.

Answers: 1. Historian 2. New Stone Age 3. Athens 4. Romans 5. Gutenberg Press

INDEX